Trevethlan

A Corni

Volu

William Davy Watson

Alpha Editions

This edition published in 2024

ISBN : 9789362094711

Design and Setting By
Alpha Editions
www.alphaedis.com
Email - info@alphaedis.com

As per information held with us this book is in Public Domain.
This book is a reproduction of an important historical work. Alpha Editions uses the best technology to reproduce historical work in the same manner it was first published to preserve its original nature. Any marks or number seen are left intentionally to preserve its true form.

Contents

VOLUME 2	- 1 -
CHAPTER I.	- 3 -
CHAPTER II.	- 9 -
CHAPTER III.	- 15 -
CHAPTER IV.	- 20 -
CHAPTER V.	- 27 -
CHAPTER VI.	- 34 -
CHAPTER VII.	- 41 -
CHAPTER VIII.	- 49 -
CHAPTER IX.	- 55 -
CHAPTER X.	- 63 -
CHAPTER XI.	- 68 -
CHAPTER XII.	- 74 -
CHAPTER XIII.	- 82 -
CHAPTER XIV.	- 91 -
CHAPTER XV.	- 96 -

VOLUME 2

CHAPTER I.

Pur' è soave cosa, a chi del tutto
Non è privo di senso, il patrio nido:
Che diè Natura al nascimento umano,
Verso il caro paese, ov' altri è nato,
Un non so che di non inteso affetto,
Che sempre vive, è non invecchia mai.

GUARINI.

Once more we stand on the shore of Mount's Bay. Far behind we have left the whirl and tumult of the metropolis, and we hear only the hoarse roar of the surges, driven by the last winds of January to beat against the granite at our feet. When last we looked over the same waters, the yellow leaves were falling from the trees, and the little waves rippled musically upon the rock, while the voice of mourning was heard in our halls. Yet if the year was declining, there was beauty in the decay; if the season was sad, there was hope amidst the sorrow. We return to find the fields desolate, and the sea tempestuous, and our house still forlorn. The face of nature is gloomy and cold, and hope has vanished from our fireside.

Such might be among the first reflections of the orphans of Trevethlan, as they gazed from the windows of the castle over the well-known landscape. They had come home, not as children from school to holiday, exulting in freedom and buoyant with hope, to exchange coercion for caresses; nor as older pupils, having learnt the value of time, merely to modify the routine of occupation, and gladden parental affection with their progress and prudence; nor yet as those who, having entered on the labour of life, know that the bow must not always be bent, and rejoice to seek relaxation around the hearth where they were nursed. Far deeper than any of these were the emotions of the sister, and dark and stern were the thoughts of the brother.

Helen's letter had fallen upon Polydore like a thunderbolt. She had, indeed, in previous communications somewhat ruffled his serenity by indistinct references to the new solicitude she detected in Randolph; but the worthy chaplain readily explained all similar hints by the novelty of his old pupil's situation. "He will become used to it before long, Mr. Griffith," Polydore would say, when the steward ventured to remind him of their difference of opinion respecting the orphans' scheme. "'Tis only the roughness of a first meeting with the world. The points will be soon rubbed smooth. There's a great difference between the Temple and Trevethlan Castle." In reply to which sort of remark, Griffith could only shrug his shoulders, and hope it might all turn out well in the end.

So when the missive arrived, in which Helen announced that her brother had proclaimed their real name, and abandoned his career, and that they should follow the letter without delay, Polydore was struck with sudden consternation. The steward was too delicate to show that he felt no similar surprise in the chaplain's presence, but to his wife he avowed that he was not in the least astonished. "A Trevethlan conceal his name!" he exclaimed. "It's not in the blood. No, Charlotte Griffith; if we are poor, we are also proud. The secret would be always on the tip of his tongue. Why, suppose he quarrelled? Not unlikely, I can tell you, in one of our house. D'ye think, Mrs. Griffith, Randolph Trevethlan would go out as Mr. Morton? Pooh! pooh!"

Mrs. Griffith rather shuddered at the idea, but she remembered sundry anecdotes of the picture gallery which forbade her to impeach the justice of her husband's position. Whatever were the cause of the return, she rejoiced at the effect, and spread the same feeling among all the little household, by her orders to prepare for the reception of her young master and mistress.

So they came. It was early in the afternoon when their chaise rattled round the green of the hamlet; but a cold sleet drove along upon the wind, and kept the villagers within doors. The folk hurried to their windows only in time to see that the carriage had passed, but the extreme rarity of such a visitation drew forth a few of the curious to gaze after the chaise, as it wound more slowly up the ascent of the base-court. Randolph lay back in his corner, gloomy and foreboding; but Helen leant forward to catch the first glimpse of an old familiar face. And Jeffrey was duly on the watch; he caught sight of the carriage as it began the ascent; he soon recognized his young lady's face at the window; the gates flew open under his hand; before the travellers had alighted at the hall-door, he had run the old flag to the top of its staff, and a faint cheer from the hamlet greeted the appearance of the well-known signal. The orphans were at home.

Anxieties and forebodings vanished for a season in the warmth of welcome. The time for questions and explanations was not arrived. Everything seemed in exactly the same order as when the brother and sister left; and were it not for the difference of the seasons—were it not that a fire crackled cheerfully in the great chimney, and that patches of snow lay on the bed of mignionette, they might have supposed a night only had elapsed since their departure. But the change in themselves told that the interval had been fraught with momentous consequences for each of them.

When the first hurry of congratulation was over, Helen retired for some confidential talk with Mrs. Griffith, and her brother accompanied the chaplain in a walk round the castle. Yes, every thing remained exactly as it was. In the library, even the volume which Randolph was reading with his instructor, "Cicero on the Art of Divination," remained on the table, as if closed but yesterday, and the subject brought a passing cloud upon his brow. The portraits in the picture-gallery showed the recent care of Mrs. Griffith.

"My mother's likeness is not here, Mr. Riches?" Randolph said abruptly, as they passed along.

The chaplain, greatly surprised, shook his head in silence.

They ascended to the battlements, and faced the inclemency of the weather. The ancient pieces of ordnance showed signs of that diligence on the part of old Jeffrey, to which Polydore had alluded in a recent letter to Hampstead. More dangerous they, perchance, to the defender than the foe.

"Is there really so much alarm in the country, my dear sir?" Randolph asked. "Are our good Jeffrey's perilous precautions in any way warranted?"

"*It fama per urbes*—you know the rest," the chaplain answered. "We will speak of it by and by."

They descended to the court-yard. If the castle was unchanged, its scanty retainers were as little altered. At the great gateway Randolph found Jeffrey pacing up and down under the arch in demi-military style, while an old-fashioned brass blunderbuss rested against the wall.

"God bless you! Master Randolph," said the old man, taking the offered hand between both of his; "and welcome back. And thanks be to Him, that if so be these walls must fall to the riff-raff from Castle Dinas, why, fall they will around a Trevethlan. But the day shall not come, while"—he caught up his piece, and suddenly discharged it in the air—"the evening gun, Master Randolph. A little too soon, and not like that as was fired in the old time. But it just serves maybe to frighten the rascals, and let 'em know old Jeffrey is awake."

Randolph thanked the trusty warder for his zeal, and expressed a hope that his forebodings might not be realized; but the sentry shook his head dolefully, and reloaded his gun, saying, "Ye might as well just keep your pistols handy, Master Randolph."

Already, even in this short perambulation, the chaplain was greatly struck by the change which he observed in his former pupil. The stripling, meditative and gentle, had become a man, haughty and impassioned. The disposition, of old plastic as wax, was now at once obstinate and capricious. The change was marked in the imperiousness of Randolph's bearing, in the curl of his lip, and the abruptness of his speech. There was no want of his former respect or affection; but it was plain that henceforth he acted on his own impulse, and was not to be swayed by those who might surround him. "Is it for good or for evil?" the chaplain asked himself, when Randolph parted from him to descend to the beach, and intimated that he wished to be alone. "Pray Heaven for good, or surely my life has been wasted."

It was becoming dusky. The sleet had passed over, and the sky was cloudless; but the blast still whistled along the sea, and brought great waves to break on the well-known promontory of rock. Randolph stood on the point, heedless of the wind and spray, and gave vent to the emotions which were struggling within his bosom.

"For what am I here?" he said. "Why have I come to my home? To bury myself amidst these gray walls, and watch the gradual ebbing of all the springs of existence? To die in sullen desolation, and find a lonely grave in yonder churchyard? Hope it not, Esther Pendarrel. Not so easily quenched is the fire within me: it may ravage all around it, but it will not smoulder away, consuming only myself. But I must be alone. My sweet sister must not be scathed by my waywardness. She will rest here, while I go forth to achieve the one purpose of my heart. Our scheme has broken to pieces, but my pledge remains. Alas, that my father should bind me by so fatal an undertaking! Yet, if Esther loved—if Esther loved——

"And thou, too, whom I never knew, of whom no trace remains in my memory, my mother! Would that thou hadst not been summoned hence so soon! Would that I had felt thy softening influence, and he learnt of thee to be merciful! Why have I thought of thee so often of late? Why has that veiled shape glided through my dreams? Wilt thou not reveal thyself to thy son? Visit me, oh my mother! fling aside the veil that hides thy face, and be a light to my soul in the darkness that surrounds it."

The muser dwelt long on this invocation, pacing to and fro on the narrow strip of rock. It was the first time he had given expression to an idea which for some while had been lurking among his thoughts. At last he looked round the sky, and saw the mild radiance of the evening star.

"Beautiful planet!" he said, "which fancy chose for the arbiter of my fate, is *she* also beholding thee? Smile upon her, fair planet, and remind her of me. Teach her to think of me, even as thou hast taught me to remember her."

Tranquillized by the reflection, Randolph returned through the deepening twilight to the castle, and joined his sister and the chaplain in a small parlour, occupying a turret that overlooked the sea. It was a favourite room. There, in the evening, Polydore described at some length the state of the adjacent country. "Discontent," he said, "was very general; not only among the miners, who thought they did not earn a just share of their labour's produce, but also among the agricultural population, who complained that wages were too low in proportion to the price of provisions. And social dissatisfaction had partly assumed the aspect of political disaffection. Agitators, strangers to the district, were said to have gone about among the people. Minor outrages had not been very rare, and expressions had been reported nearly equivalent to the 'Guerre aux Châteaux' of the great French Revolution. Musters of men in military array were said to have been held on the moorlands. Rumours flew about of the landing of arms on different parts of the coast. But all," Polydore concluded, "is vague and shadowy. I believe there is great exaggeration abroad. Positive, however, it is, that a patrol of cavalry occasionally dashes at speed by a lonely cottage, and that the coast-guard display unwonted activity. Behold the confirmation of my words!"

For while they were being uttered, his hearers might see a long line of fire rise into the air from the shore of the bay near Mousehole, denoting the flight of a rocket.

"That is the way they amuse us almost every night," continued the chaplain. "'Tis too dark, I suppose, to see anything afloat. Let us put the candles in the shade, and look."

So said, so done. Fruitlessly, for they could discover nothing on the dark waters. But while they were gazing across the bay, a faint, rushing sound fell on their ear, above the noise of the sea; and, turning hastily, they perceived the last sparks of a second rocket, which had been fired from their own coast.

"Yes, that is the way," Polydore repeated. "Of old, the folks would just have wished the smuggler luck, and perhaps turned out in hope to run a keg or so; but they seem to think there's more in these signals now."

"And you feel no alarm yourself, my dear sir?" Helen inquired.

"None, Helen," replied the chaplain. "I may be mistaken, but I do not expect to see Jeffrey's blunderbuss brought into action; and I have a trust which never yet proved wanting."

So saying, Polydore rang the bell, a summons which speedily assembled all the household for family prayer, according to old usage; and when the rite was over, the members sought their respective resting-places, and silence reigned in the castle.

But Randolph could not sleep. Throwing a cloak around him, and shading his lamp with his hand, he proceeded with the stealthy step of one who dreads he knows not what, along the desolate corridors to the state apartments. Through their faded grandeur he wandered on, until he reached the great chamber which was the scene of his father's death. He placed his light so that only a faint glimmer fell upon the bed, and leant against one of the pillars, and resumed his reverie of the afternoon with such vividness of imagination, that he fancied he again beheld the bright eyes of the dying man, and heard the injunctions which seemed now to separate him from what he held dearest upon earth. But his reverie had not terminated with those gloomy forebodings, nor did his dream. A frail and slender form, veiled in gossamer-like drapery, bent dimly over the couch for a short space and floated away, beckoning him to follow. It rested a moment in the doorway, for he had only obeyed the sign with his eyes. But when he hastily seized the lamp, it flitted fast before him, fading and fading away, until it disappeared entirely as he crossed the threshold of his own chamber. He flung himself on his bed, and closed his eyes for sleep; and as the last gleam of consciousness vanished, a face which he appeared to have known in days long past, meek and lovely,—that of a woman, in her morning of beauty,— bent down upon his, and kissed his lips.

The kiss seemed yet fresh upon them when he woke, and found the sun shining gaily into the apartment.

CHAPTER II.

The intelligible forms of ancient poets,
The fair humanities of old religion,
The Power, the Beauty, and the Majesty,
That had their haunts in dale, or piny mountain,
Or forest by slow stream, or pebbly spring,
Or chasms and watery depths—all these have vanished.
They live no longer in the faith of reason.

COLERIDGE. *Piccolomini.*

The hamlet of Trevethlan nestled snugly under the slope, at the summit of which stood the castle, and was screened by the rising ground from the sea breezes. It surrounded a green of limited extent, which was only separated from the base-court by the gate Michael Sinson opened for Mrs. Pendarrel's carriage, when that lady was returning from her frustrated attack. On the right, a small wicket led into the churchyard, so full of trees that, except at the present season, the church itself could scarcely be seen. This was a plain edifice, with no pretensions to beauty, deriving all its picturesqueness from the ivy with which it was overgrown. Opposite to it, across the green, a beam projecting from the front of an old-fashioned house, supported the escutcheon of the lords of the village, and, by its inscription, promised good entertainment to man and beast. But the inn had shared the fortunes of the castle: the windows of the wings, which advanced with scalloped gables beyond the centre, were blocked up with boards, and the middle part only appeared to be now occupied. But Dame Miniver, the hostess, had inherited the savings of more prosperous days. She was a trim, bustling widow woman, tidy and rosy, notable and talkative, whose only sighs were divided between the good-man who slept on the other side of the green, and the splendour which had departed from the castle on the cliff. She never fretted because her stables now held none but a few farm horses, nor because there were no longer any swaggering lackeys to come and crack a bottle of the port, some of which might still be slumbering in her cellars. She would hardly have been a Cornish woman if she did not know how to exchange a wink with the good fellow who had a keg of hollands or brandy to dispose of; and it pleased her mightily to treat a revenue man with a drop of the spirits that had been run under his very nose.

The other habitations surrounding the green were of various sizes, some with small gardens in front, some neat, and some neglected,—almost all thatched and whitewashed. A sleepy, listless air hung about the place. A stranger wandering accidentally into it, would feel at once that it had known better days; the children might seem to play with less liveliness than usual, and the very geese to waddle over the grass with a lazy gait. He would fancy the gossips at the cottage doors to be inanimate in their chat, and might himself be yielding to a sense of drowsiness, when the sight of Dame Miniver, in her neat brown silk gown, and snow-white apron, looking complacently at the visitor, with an inviting smile that was irresistible, would recall his fleeting spirits, and guide his steps to the friendly shelter of the Trevethlan Arms.

The late owner of the castle, it has already been said, was extremely unpopular with his tenantry, for some time both before and after his marriage. Proud themselves of the family upon which they had depended beyond the memory of man, they hated to see it stripped, acre by acre, of its broad lands, and so impoverished as to be unable to afford them the old advantages. Remembering the current prophecy, they loathed a match which seemed to harbinger its fulfilment, and at the same time rendered it next to impossible for Pendarrel to come to Trevethlan, although the reverse might happen on several contingencies. But after the death of poor Margaret, and when an infant son and daughter stood in the way of any such consummation, and their lord came often among them, haughty indeed, but not unkind; poor, but still generous; and they could not avoid seeing the melancholy written in his face, and recollected his reported courtship, years before, of Esther Pendarrel, and thought of the kinsman who had sold his name; their animosity gradually melted into compassion, and a deep and sullen hatred grew up among them against the house of Pendarrel and everything connected with it.

The discontent now pervading the country had not spared Trevethlan. It was true, that if the sentiment—war to the mansions—were diffused at all in the village, it had no reference to the castle. There was not a man on the estate but was ready to die in defence of the towers on the cliff. But other feelings might be entertained towards some of their neighbours. Hitherto they had exhausted their animosity in conflicts arising at wrestling-matches and country fairs, but now there were symptoms discoverable of more dangerous hostilities.

And the movement was encouraged by the absence of the young master. The villagers regretted, without blaming, a departure which was intended, they hoped, in some way or other, to restore prosperity to the family. But it removed a check which might have soothed their exasperation. And in like manner the return of the orphans would probably turn aside any ideas of immediate violence, if such had really gained any footing in the hamlet.

On the evening of their arrival, some of the notables met to discuss things in general, around the fire in Dame Miniver's hall. There were farmer Colan, and Germoe the tailor of the hamlet, and Breage whose wife kept the shop where everything was sold, and, among divers others, Edward Owen, Sinson's unsuccessful rival for the affections of pretty Mercy Page. Owen, formerly one of the best-conducted men in the hamlet, was now sulky and perverse, and Mercy had obtained no slight odium by her too great fidelity to one who was regarded as a deserter. She little thought her old lover had been lately in the neighbourhood, and she was even now meditating an excursion to inquire after him, in one of those mysterious modes, which were yet resorted to occasionally by the lovers of the far-west.

"A health to our squire!" cried Colan, filling a cup of cyder, "and to our bonny young lady, and welcome back to Trevethlan."

"Faith," said Owen, "they're not come back to do much good to Trevethlan, I reckon. There's none of the fortune come with 'em as folks used to talk about, or they'd never ha' gone through the town with a rubbishy old chay from Helston."

"Small blame to Squire Randolph," observed Germoe, "that he don't throw away the little he's left, like our poor master before him. And, for my part, I'd rather have him among us, poor though he may be, than away nobody knows where.

'The place is bare, when the lord's not there.'

There'll be more smiles in Trevethlan than there's been this many a day."

"Then there's not much to smile about," Owen replied; "and the best maybe the squire could do, were to take back some of that's been stolen from him. There's many a lad ready to strike a blow for Trevethlan."

"Wild talk, Edward," said Breage; "wild talk, and nothing but it. We live by the law now-a-days."

"And there's a pleasanter way," observed Dame Miniver. "Miss Mildred of Pendar'l 's as pretty a lady as ever stepped, and she might bring the squire all his land again, and fulfil the saying quite agreeable,

'Pendar'l and Trevethlan will own one name.'"

"There's too much ill blood atween the houses," Colan said. "A deal too much. Didn't the lady of Pendar'l turn the late squire away? And didn't our young master send her back from his gate with a flea in her ear? Don't ye recollect how Jeffrey chuckled about it? The young folks have ne'er seen one another, Mrs. Miniver."

"How d'ye know?" the hostess asked. "And trust me, if meet they did, there'd meet a couple predestinated to fall in love. In all the old tales that ever I read, the true gentleman falls in love with the wrong lady. But, of course, they must meet, or they haven't the chance, and somehow they always do meet."

"Well," said Germoe, "I'll wager the day ne'er dawns that sees that match. The saying'll not hold good in our time—mark my words."

"There's a deal of wisdom in those old sayings," quoth Mistress Miniver. "Ay, and in others too. Mind ye not how old Maud Basset foretold a fortune for her child, and the gipsy crossed it, and both came out as true as gospel? Those sayings are not to be looked down upon, Master Germoe."

"If ever that saying comes true in my time," muttered Owen, "and not on our side, there'll be a tale told of Pendar'l—that's all I know."

But the remark excited no attention, and from such predictions the company slid by degrees into the kindred and fascinating subject of preternatural visitations, a wide field in that remote district of the west; and they drew their seats closer round the fire, and dropped their voices, until they almost frightened one another into a reluctance to separate on their different ways homeward.

They would, perhaps, have expressed themselves in a more discontented manner, if they had known the intention with which Randolph sought the home of his fathers: he has himself obscurely intimated it, in his soliloquy by the sea. To persuade his sister to remain in those old halls, under the guardianship of Polydore Riches; to return himself to London, to obtain, in spite of all obstacles, an interview with Mildred Pendarrel; to extract from her the confession which he was convinced she was ready to make; to exchange mutual vows; to look round the world for the path which he might cut to honour and fortune; to return and claim his bride, who by that time would be her own mistress—such was the scheme upon which he was at present resolved. It was a wild outline, and he did not trouble himself to fill up the details. Young and ardent, he looked straight to the summit of his ambition, and recked nothing of the ravines which separated the various intervening ridges.

But with all his determination he hesitated to disclose his idea to Helen. He felt that to her he was everything. Until quite recently they had always shared one another's thoughts. He trembled at the anguish he should inflict by such a separation. And so he deferred the confidence from time to time, persuading himself that it would best be made on the very eve of his departure, until this was indefinitely postponed by intelligence that Pendarrel Hall was being prepared for the immediate reception of its mistress.

In the meanwhile his sister and he renewed their former acquaintance with the good folks of the hamlet, and to external appearance resumed the way in which they had lived before the late Mr. Trevethlan's death. It was a quiet, dreamy sort of life, of which a faint sketch was given in the outset of this narrative. They were born in a land of romance; the whole region was classic ground. From King Arthur's castle of Tintagel in the north-east, to Merlin's stone in Mount's Bay, respecting which an old prophecy—

"There shall land on the stone Merlyn
Those shall burn Paul's, Penzance, and Newlyn,"

was said to be fulfilled by some stragglers from the Spanish Armada, every field might be supposed the scene of some chivalrous exploit, or magical enchantment, or superstitious sacrifice. There dwelt the last of the British druids: their strange monuments were still standing on the wild moors and in the cultivated domains, on the desolate carns and among the crags of the sea-shore. Such was the oracular stone at Castle Trereen,—at that time not forced from its resting-place by sacrilegious hands, and requiring no chain to keep it from *logging* too far. Such was Lanyon Quoit, a cromlech on the moorland beyond Madron, and not very far from the battle-field, where the Saxon Athelstan finally defeated the Britons, and drove them to perish of hunger in the caves of Pendeen. The curious stranger still marks their strong fortresses, Castle Chun and Castle Dinas, occupying the highest ground between Mount's Bay and the Irish Sea; he may read the name of their chieftain, Rialobran, on his tombstone, Mên Skryfa, now prostrate among the herbage; and he may note the sanguinary nature of the struggle, in the title which it gained for the Land's End, of Penvonlas, or the Headland of Blood.

And, again, the customs of the country still kept alive some faint memorials of those heathen times, and of the accommodating spirit of the earliest Christian missionaries. To such an origin is ascribed the salutation of the orchards at Christmas, already referred to: the mistletoe of the apple was not so sacred as that of the oak, but neither was it despicable. And the bonfires of St. John's Eve were said to tell of the days when the cromlechs of Cam Brey were surrounded by a mystic grove, and the officiating priests hurried their human victims through purifying flames to the blood-stained altar.

Nor was the land less indebted for romantic associations to those fabulous historians, who peopled Britain with royalty, beauty, chivalry, and faery, and assigned to Cornwall the honour of producing the renowned Sir Tristan. Not a few hours were whiled away at Trevethlan Castle in discoursing of their marvellous adventures, their strange wandering towns of Camelot and Caerleon, and the general phantasmagoric character of their narratives. They plotted out the kingdom in an imaginary map, and whatever scenery they required, they regarded as existing and well known. Did they want a lake, from whence should issue a hand bearing a magic sword, they troubled not themselves with any mention of its landmarks: a forest perilous arose wherever they willed: a bridge to be defended, and therefore a stream, was always ready in the champion's path: you were introduced to a fountain as if you had drunk at it all your life. Undoubting faith in their own story was one of their most powerful fascinations: it transferred itself to their hearers, and a tale, which modern exactness would make incoherent and incredible, became credible from its very indistinctness. The Round Table romances present us with a fantastic Britain, which we may conceive to be still in being, like the paradise of Irem in the desert of Aden, and which the second-sight of imagination may yet conjure up in all its pristine glory.

Many of those old tomes, quartos and folios, whose florid binding attested their high estimation by early possessors, enriched the shelves of the castle library; and few of its proprietors were deterred from exploring their contents, by the mystic black-letter and antiquated French in which the stories were told. Under Polydore's guidance, Randolph and Helen had become acquainted with much of this legendary lore; and even their father sometimes deigned to take part in a conversation arising out of it.

But it was in vain now that Helen, in the hope of chasing away the cloud which hung continually upon her brother's brow, strove to recall his attention to these studies of the old time. The down had been brushed from the butterfly's wing. She strolled with him along the beach, and she sat with him in Merlin's Cave, in spite of the wintry weather; but it was impossible to bring back the mood in which he listened to "Trevethlan's farewell," on the eve of their departure for London. He was fond of roaming through the desolate state rooms, rapt in deep meditation, and only roused when the wind, rushing through some crevice, waved the tapestry of the walls with a rustling sound, and made the dim figures portrayed upon it seem for a moment endued with life. Sometimes he would be found in the picture-gallery, gazing earnestly on the portrait of his father, and seeming, by the expression of his countenance, eager to evoke from the mimic lips an answer to some question which was struggling in his breast. His old teacher noted his moodiness with anxiety, but in silence, and made no attempt to forestall the explanation, which he felt sure must come of itself before long.

CHAPTER III.

The heart, surrendered to the ruling power
Of some ungoverned passion every hour,
Finds, by degrees, the truths that once bore sway
And all their deep impression wear away:
So coin grows smooth in traffic current passed,
Till Cæsar's image is effaced at last.

COWPER.

The mistress of Pendarrel Hall never visited it without experiencing a renewal of many an ancient spring of grief. There were not a few spots in the park, sequestered from the more frequented paths, which she could not look upon without bitter regret, yet which she was always sure to explore within a few days of her arrival, so much of pensive pleasure mingled with the pain. But the influence of such reminiscences was of short duration, and the temporary weakness was soon succeeded by that permanent animosity to the owners of Trevethlan Castle, which had become the ruling passion of her life. She would climb an eminence in the neighbourhood, from which the old gray towers were visible, and think, with fresh exasperation, of the obstinacy or the pride which still detained them from her grasp.

But now she came to her home, with a fond belief that the enemy was at last delivered into her hand. Previously, there seemed no limit to the contention. Now, a few weeks must decide it. Michael Sinson had returned to town before the departure of his patroness, had matured his plans, had obtained her sanction to carrying them out, and had been introduced by her husband to his highly-respected solicitor, Mr. Truby. That gentleman could only assure his client, after a careful perusal of Sinson's statement, that, if it did not break down in court, there could be no doubt whatever that Mr. Randolph Trevethlan would be held to be an intruder upon the castle property, and that immediate possession would be given to him, Mr. Trevethlan Pendarrel. And, as Michael vouched for the perfect soundness of his evidence, Mr. Truby received directions to commence proceedings forthwith. "Let the suit be pressed forward," Mrs. Pendarrel said, "with the utmost possible despatch."

That matter settled, she left London with her daughter; her husband gladly making his official duties a plea for remaining in May Fair. Yet Esther was not altogether at her ease. Plain and straightforward as was Sinson's story, and completely as it destroyed the validity of the late Mr. Trevethlan's marriage, she still suspected there was some unseen flaw. She often thought of Mr. Truby's qualification—if the case did not break down in court. Who was this very important witness that Sinson had so opportunely discovered? And then, as the notion of fraud stole into her mind, she asked herself, what would be the motive; with what object could Sinson have devised his scheme? And again she questioned herself, with some alarm, as to the extent to which she had authorized the proceedings of her protégé. She had communicated with him once or twice by letter. And the uneasiness expressed in these reflections was somewhat increased by Michael's recent demeanour. He wore a look of intelligence, and assumed an air of importance, seeming to discover a consciousness of some hidden power. A sense of superiority appeared to mingle with his fawning subserviency, such as might mark the carriage of Luke in Massinger's play. But Mrs. Pendarrel soon wrapped herself in her pride, and forgot all her suspicions.

To be sure, that pride rather revolted from the mode of proceeding. An action-at-law was but a bad substitute for a raid of the olden time. The bailiff with a slip of parchment was an indifferent representative of a "plump of spears." The court was but a poor arena, compared to the lists. But for this there was no help. The inconvenient civilization of modern times precluded a resort to that picturesque method of settling the question. And Mrs. Pendarrel owned to herself that her husband was but ill-qualified to head a foray. She recollected the pretences by which he had obtained her hand, and confessed that he would cut a bitter figure in "Doe on the demise of Pendarrel against Trevethlan," than in a cartel of mortal defiance.

Yet had she good cause to tremble. She had only discerned one-half of Sinson's character, his malice against the Trevethlans. She employed him in a manner which gratified that feeling, and she supposed her pecuniary favours were sufficient to make him her own. But he was far from being a slave, like an eastern mute, or a messenger of the Vehm-Gericht, who would answer in humble submission, "to hear is to obey:" he had his own game to play beside that of his mistress, and well would it be for her if she did not lose more than she won by his cunning finesse.

His disposition had been nourished by his whole life. His early years were spent in the most abject servility. He fawned upon his young cousin, the heir of Trevethlan, like a spaniel. To obtain his partiality, and to be admitted to his society, he was ready to lick the dust under his feet. And at the same time he thought, or was persuaded by his grandmother, that the ties of blood made such distinction a matter of right rather than of favour. So very early in life he acquired ideas much above his real station, and pined for a position for which he was not born.

When Randolph's father ejected the young rustic from the castle, this aspiring ambition seemed to be nipped in the bud. The disappointment was very severe, and his fanatical grandmother changed it into hatred. Having been urgent in inducing her daughter to accept the offered elevation, she heard of the treatment portrayed in poor Margaret's fading cheek with wrath, and regarded her death as a murder to be avenged. So she trained Michael as the instrument of retribution, and made his personal spite the basis of a deep-rooted animosity against all the house of Trevethlan.

With such feelings he presented himself to Mrs. Pendarrel, and was received into her service. And well pleased he was to find that his first duties implied more or less of hostility towards his former playmate. He entered upon the task with a zeal inspired by hatred. The departure of the orphans from their home seemed to deprive him of his occupation, but in fact widened its sphere. The summons to London extended the bounds of the young peasant's ambition. He had profited well by the early instructions of Polydore Riches; he was of good figure, with a handsome, if unprepossessing face; a short residence in the metropolis changed his rusticity into assurance; and his natural abilities qualified him to play many parts, and in some degree to seem a gentleman.

His progress was quickened by the glimpse he caught of Miss Pendarrel at his first arrival in town. It developed a series of sensations in his mind, only partially excited before by the rural charms of Mercy Page, and made him feel the inferiority of his station with tenfold bitterness. He thought vaguely of Sir Richard Whittington and Sir Ralph Osborne, and longed for the opportunity of making a rapid fortune. With this idea, he bought a ticket in the lottery.

And as he advanced in the confidence of his patroness, a new prospect opened before him. He fancied he saw the means of obtaining a control over her, by which he could bend her to his will, whenever the time came. So that he reached his end, he cared not for the road. And in this case every passion of his heart concurred in urging him forward. Circumstances favoured his desires even beyond his expectations, and the period was approaching to strike the final blow.

Sinson's connection with the wretched spendthrift, Everope, has already been traced. He destined that individual to play an important part in his plot. The miserable man hung back at every step, and ended by clearing it. Michael's money supplied him with dissipation, and in dissipation he drowned remorse. But the trip into the country nearly rescued him from his betrayer's clutches; it had given him time for reflection such as he had not had for many a day; and when on their return, Sinson laid open his further demands, he encountered a resistance so obstinate that he almost thought his previous labour had been thrown away. But threats and temptations did their work, and Everope finally agreed to take the step, which Sinson promised should be the last required of him. And now Michael remained in town, instead of at once accompanying his patroness to Pendarrel, in order to furnish Mr. Truby with information, and to take heed that his reluctant dupe did not slip through his fingers.

The second week in February had scarcely begun, when Esther arrived in Cornwall. Well might Gertrude warn Mildred that she underrated the difficulties of her position. Mrs. Pendarrel treated her with the most tender consideration, but with great art made her constantly feel that the marriage was a settled thing, without ever affording her an opportunity of protesting. Her assent was continually implied, yet in such a way that she could not contradict the inference. Her situation became embarrassing and irksome. It was ungenerous, she thought, to take such an advantage of maidenly scruples. She felt that a web was being spun round her, reducing her to a sort of chrysalis, from which it was every day harder to escape, but from which she was resolved a fly should issue, by no means like what was expected.

For she entertained no fear about the final result. If her mother chose to go on, wilfully blind, from day to day, without permitting her eyes to be opened, on her must rest the blame of any éclat. The remembrance of her cousin was deeply imprinted on her heart, and sustained its courage. Night after night, before retiring to rest, she drew aside the curtains of her window to look for the bright planet which he had associated with his destiny, saddened when it was hidden by clouds or dimmed by mist, happy when its rays beamed pure and clear into her chamber.

There were no guests staying at the hall, but numbers of casual visitors called to pay their respects, and hoped perhaps for an invitation to the wedding. And notes, of all shapes and sizes, requested the honour ... at dinner and at dance. And a gay life would Mildred's have been, but that she was so preoccupied. For her mother accepted nearly all the proffered hospitality, and returned it with liberal profusion. And at every one of these festive meetings, Mildred could see that in the compliments Mrs. Pendarrel received, and in her furtive and complacent answers, she had no small portion.

One source of comfort she had, that Melcomb was not in the country. She had not to endure his odious addresses. But her mother had issued cards for a grand entertainment at rather a distant date, when she hoped to crowd her house with everybody who was the least presentable in all West Kerrier, and to that high festival Mildred feared he would come, an undesired guest, and be in some way exhibited as her accepted suitor to the assembled multitude. But the day was yet far off.

And it was with pleasure she learnt that Randolph and his sister had returned to their ancestral home. Much speculation was afloat concerning them; and though people generally knew the family disagreement, and refrained from alluding to them in Mrs. Pendarrel's presence, slight hints fell inadvertently at times; and some mean minds, little knowing the nature of her they addressed, uttered a passing sarcasm upon their poverty, with the notion that it would be agreeable. But to Mildred the mere mention of their name was a source of interest; and in her rural walks she would sometimes inquire concerning them of the country folk, and speculate on the possibility of meeting Randolph on her way.

To her mother their presence was not equally agreeable. She was far from anxious for any such rencontre. She too well remembered the emotion displayed by Mildred at Mrs. Winston's. She learnt, with regret, that the orphans did not lead so absolutely sequestered a life as before their father's death; but availed themselves of the removal of the restriction which then confined their walks to the precincts of the castle and the sea coast, and made themselves in some measure acquainted with the wild scenery surrounding their native bay. She did not like the idea of being so near them, just at the time when Sinson's machinations were about to explode. And with a different interest she heard of the state of feeling manifested pretty openly by the tenantry of Trevethlan, and desired her protégé to come to Pendarrel as soon as he should be released from attendance on Mr. Truby. She wished to have more precise information of what passed in the castle and its dependent hamlet, and summoned her retainer to resume his original occupation.

CHAPTER IV.

Tu ne quæsieris, scire nefas, quem mihi, quem tibi
Finem Di dederint, Leuconoc; nec Babylonios
Tentaris numeros. Ut melius, quidquid erit, pati!

Hor.

Seek not to know, it is not given,
The end for us ordained by Heaven;
Nor be by fortune-tellers lured:
What can't be cured, is best endured.

Madron church-town, the mother of the thriving port of Penzance, is a small irregular hamlet, situated on an eminence overlooking its well-grown offspring, and the salt marshes which skirt the coast in the direction of Marazion. It is approached by a steep and winding road, but the prospect from the churchyard will well repay the labour of the way. And many a pilgrim, when he turns from the landscape spread beneath to the memorials at his feet, and feels the breeze from the sea breathe lightly over his cheek, will be mournfully reminded how many have sought a refuge on that genial shore from our English destroyer, beguiling themselves and those dear to them, with the hope of eluding his pursuit, but sinking, nevertheless, under his ruthless embrace; for on the tombstones round him the stranger will read of other strangers, from far distant places, with names unknown to Cornwall, once graced, he may imagine, with youth and beauty, of whose history it is there written that they "came to Penzance for the benefit of their health." Those simple words, repeated on every side, tell the melancholy end of many a romance.

Up the hill, on an early day in February, a trim country girl was climbing with a step that betokened some indecision of purpose. She was dressed in a dark blue frock, short and full in the skirt, and a red cloak of scanty dimensions, which hung over one shoulder and under the other arm. She was hot, and carried her bonnet, decked with some of the first primroses of the year, in her hand, while her black hair hung round a pair of bright eyes of the same colour, and cheeks always red, and now redder than usual. A very pretty rustic was Mercy Page.

It is some four miles from Marazion to Madron, and further still from Trevethlan; but that is not much for a Cornish maiden. Mercy had walked all the way. But she had not walked with the free quick step usual to her, nor did their wonted open smile play round her provoking lips. Her look was anxious, and her pace uncertain. And now that she was toiling up the hill, and perhaps approaching her destination, she not unfrequently stopped, and with her finger in the corner of her mouth, tried to scrutinize herself, while she seemed to be regarding the prospect. For Mercy had a kind of idea that she was on her way to do what was at least foolish, if not wrong, and she had always been a very good girl.

But with all this hesitation, she still advanced. She crossed Madron churchyard, and went out of her way to drop a flower on the grave of a cousin who lay there, making a longer pause on the occasion than any which had previously interrupted her walk. However, she proceeded at last, and soon turned aside from the main road by a tiny streamlet. She followed the rivulet's course, as it wound along beneath a bank covered in the summer with broom, gorse, and heather, from amidst which, here and there, a graceful silver birch flung its long tresses on the breeze, until she arrived at a sort of bay or inlet, where the trees grew more thickly, and in the very depth of which lay, still, silent, and dark, encircled by rude stone-work, a well of water, the source of the streamlet which had guided the maiden's steps—St. Madron's Well.

Mercy cast a sharp glance before her, and was glad to see that there was no person near the fountain. She went up to it herself, and bent over the mirror-like surface, and might see her image rising dimly to meet the salute. Could that limpid water tell a maiden's fortune? Was it conscious of the reflection of her features? Could it read their gentle lines, and foreshow by any ripple of its own, the destiny of her who looked upon it? And was such inquiry sanctioned by the saint who had blessed the fountain? Was it not profane so to forestall futurity? Such questions flitted vaguely through Mercy's bosom while she gazed into the tranquil well. An expression of awe stole over her face; and when, as she changed her position, a straggling briar which had caught her cloak twitched it, she started like a guilty thing, and turned suddenly with a flush on her cheeks and forehead, deeper even than that called forth by exercise. She did not smile on discovering the source of her alarm, but began to search among the pebbles of the brook for some smoother and rounder than common. Having collected two or three of this description, she returned to the fountain, and from trembling fingers, and with eyes half afraid to watch the result, dropped one of the stones into the water. There was a little splash, and then the circling wavelets grew larger and larger, and broke against the sides of the well, and a new ripple arose from each point of contact, and the undulations crossed one another in every direction, and became fainter and fainter, until the surface once more motionless, again presented the maiden with the semblance of her own pretty features, just as she saw them before the disturbance.

Was Mercy any the wiser? She drew a long breath, and murmured to herself, "he is not———" She had heard that if the well were unruffled, the oracle pronounced the person inquired of to be dead. The oracle, it may be presumed, was generally favourable to hope. But Mercy wished to learn much more than this; and those changing and intermingling ripples had to her been as hieroglyphics to the eyes of the profane. She dropped another of her pebbles into the well. Again the same sight, and the same disappointment. Vainly did Mercy try to shape the little waves into words, or letters, or symbols. She could not make out even a "yes" or a "no." Once more she tried the experiment, and becoming more enthusiastic, pressed the pebble to her lips before she let it fall.

Still it was all the same. The oracle was dumb. Mercy was inclined to revile St. Madron. She had grown excited; felt reconciled to the practice of the black art, and ventured on a step, which, when she started from home, she vowed to herself nothing should induce her to take.

There was a cottage, or rather a hovel, which the maiden had passed on her way to the well, and which she had shunned. The bank formed one of its sides, and it was hard to say where the ground ended and the dwelling began. The walls were built of rough stones, the interstices between them being filled with moss, which had accepted the employment willingly, and grown and flourished. The roof also was of turf, and thus the abode had a vegetable aspect, and looked like an unusually large clump of green, such as one sees often on a moist common, tempting one's foot to press it, or suggesting the idea of an unpleasantly soft pillow. This was the nest of Dame Gudhan, the self-constituted priestess of St. Madron's Well. She was a toothless, deformed, ugly old woman, who lived with her cat, which she had succeeded in training to poach, and bring the game it killed home to be cooked, instead of wasting it raw in the open field. Friend she had none but pussy, but she enjoyed a high reputation as a witch; and many a girl travelled many a mile to ascertain from Dame Gudhan the colour of her future's hair and eyes, and all his other good qualities.

Now the sibyl had observed the detour which Mercy made to avoid passing near her hut, and observed it with due professional pique. To consult the spirit of the well without the assistance of its minister was to defraud the latter of her rightful perquisite, and depreciate the science of witchcraft. So, whenever Dame Gudhan perceived a timid devotee steal furtively to the well, she would lie in wait for her return, and favour her with unsought predictions of a nature less agreeable than strong. Eying Mercy from the door of her den, the old hag thought her appearance indicated one quite able to afford a fee, and proportionate to the idea was the sibylline wrath. But in order to increase her anger to the proper pitch, Dame Gudhan trod hard upon her cat's tail; and the animal, resenting the affront, inflicted a long scratch upon its mistress's shin. Thereupon ensued a hideous war; a yelling as of the evil demons with which the pythoness pretended to be familiar; unintelligible to vulgar ears; requiring an interpreter from the oyster-quays. It may be supposed the witch had the best of the argument, for after a while, pussy issued from the hovel with her tail trailing behind her, and trotted off in a crest-fallen fashion, stopping now and then to look round sulkily, and shake her whiskers with impotent spite.

Dame Gudhan speedily followed grimalkin, tottering along on a stick, and muttering to herself, chewing her rage as a horse champs the bit. She encountered Mercy at the opening which led to the well.

"Didst read he would be hung, lass?" she squealed, while all the muscles of her yellow wrinkled visage twitched frightfully. "Didst read he would be hung?"

With all her heart Mercy wished herself safe back at Trevethlan.

"Dost tremble?" continued Dame Gudhan. "What wilt do when the day comes? There's murder in thy face—a red spot on thy brow."

Poor Mercy gasped for breath, and leaned against the bank. She had thrust her hand into her pocket, but was too much agitated to find what she wanted. The old crone divined her intention.

"Na," she screamed. "The spirit won't be bought. The cord's about thy neck, and the gibbet's reared for him. The tree grows no more in the wood. It is felled, and hewn, and squared. The hemp is reaped, and beat, and spun. In an evil day came ye to the blessed well, and passed by Dame Gudhan without seeking her advice. Said is said."

By this time Mercy had succeeded in producing a little purse of red leather with a steel clasp. Her fingers shook very much as she opened it, and tendered Dame Gudhan a bright new shilling, its sole contents. The hag was satisfied with the effect of her fierce prophecy—one she had often vented on like occasions, and looked at the coin with greedy eyes, chattering her teeth, and smacking her lips.

"That was his new-year's gift, I reckon," she said.

She was wrong, and the mistake restored Mercy's fleeting courage.

"Take it, dame," said the maiden.

"Ye'll lack a new ribbon at Sithney fair. And what for? Said is said."

It was a fine instance of conscientious scruples, that affected reluctance of the old woman to receive the maiden's money.

"Take it, dame," Mercy repeated.

"The spirit never lies," said the hag, taking the shilling; "but he sometimes explains his words. Come ye back to the well. Said is said. We'll ask him what it means."

So saying, she hobbled on her stick up the little dell. Mercy looked after her doubtfully, and was more than inclined to walk rapidly away; but, yielding to the fascination which commonly attends inquiries like hers, she at last followed the old crone, and overtook her at the well.

"Now, lass," said the enchantress, "an evil rede I read ye but now, and evil it may be. But forewarned is forearmed. Ye need na be frightened. And so ye saw nought in the dark water. Ye could na hear his voice. Ye kenned na whether he laughed or frowned, or promised or threatened. Smooth and still, deep and dark. Reach me thy hand. Stand by my side, and when I press thy fingers, then drop the pebble."

Injunctions which the maiden obeyed with tremulous emotion. The old hag knelt down by the fountain-side, and bent over the water until she nearly touched it with her lips, mumbling some incantation. Suddenly she squeezed Mercy's hand in her grasp, and the maiden let fall the pebble which she held in the other. At the sound of the splash the witch raised her head a little, and seemed to scan the ripples which circled on the surface of the well. It was only for a moment, and then she started to her feet, dashed a handful of water in Mercy's face, and screamed:

"Wash it off, wash it off. The spirit never lies. Said is said. Away, lass; away."

She waved Mercy off, and the maiden retreated backwards before her, step by step, until she reached the lower end of the ravine, unable to remove her eyes from those of the fortune-teller. On the open ground Dame Gudhan passed her without uttering another word, and hobbled quickly away to her wretched abode, taking no notice of her cat, which had now returned home, and appeared disposed to make up the late quarrel by purring and rubbing against the old woman's wounded shin.

Mercy, exhausted and terrified, watched her until she disappeared within her dwelling, and then, feeling relieved from her presence, and moved by a sudden impulse, she dropped on her knees and implored, in her own homely manner, the forgiveness of Heaven for what she had just done. She rose somewhat tranquillized, and took her way homeward with a quick step.

Fortune-tellers, unlike Dame Gudhan, generally give good tidings, and in the few cases where it is otherwise, they are disbelieved. Were it not so, the trade would be ruined. People forebode quite sufficient evil for themselves, and seek a conjuror for comfort, not for aggravation of their uneasiness. A strange fatuity it is that prompts such attempts to raise the veil which hides the future! Were the object accomplished life would be valueless; its interest would be gone; there would be nothing left to live for, and we should be unable to die; we should be fatalists by experience. The impatient reader, who peruses the last chapter of the novel first, has still to learn in what manner the author educes his catastrophe; but the miserable victim of foresight would be acquainted, not only with the close, but with all the incidents of his coming career. And difficult it is to see how human strength could bear up against such a certainty, where the vision was of ill. So the inquirer is apt to discredit the information which he came to seek, when it proves to be unfavourable to his desires.

Mercy Page, already fortified by her silent prayer, soon regained her ordinary cheerfulness. Her spirits rose as she walked, and she tripped lightly along, in happy forgetfulness of Dame Gudhan's frightful denunciations. So she passed under the pretty hamlet of Gulvall, with its picturesque church-tower peeping forth from the embosoming trees, and descended to the hard sands of the sea-shore. For the tide was out, and the beach afforded a short cut to Marazion. Blithely and briskly the maiden sped over the ribbed plain, until she saw in the distance, advancing to meet her, a figure which she recognized.

At that moment there was no individual, perhaps, whom Mercy less desired to see than Edward Owen, her discarded suitor. The woman cannot be worth winning who takes pleasure in rejecting an honest admirer, and Mercy was not a village coquette. She sincerely regretted that Owen's attachment could only be a source of sorrow to himself. She deplored it the more, because the disappointment seemed to have driven the lover into some irregular courses. Now Mercy had sought St. Madron's Well with a vague idea of confirming her belief in the fidelity of a more favoured suitor; and, passing by the rude shock of her interview with Dame Gudhan, it was not on her return from such an errand that she was pleased to meet his rival. Meet him, however, she must, and did.

"A bright evening to you, Mercy," Owen said, as they approached one another; "though bright there is nothing for me. And where mayst have been this fine afternoon?"

It was an awkward question for the girl. She answered it with another.

"Where are you going, Edward, with the sun behind St. Paul's, and your back to Trevethlan? It should not be a long walk ye are starting on. Better maybe to turn back with me, and walk home together."

"Mercy," said the young man, "there was a time when my heart would have jumped at the word. It is gone. I have other thoughts now. Where am I going? By Castle Dinas to St. Ives. There will be some talk in the country before long."

"What for, Edward?" Mercy asked. "They tell me I have scorned you into wild ways. I never scorned you, Edward. It is not fair of you to bring such a saying upon me. I wish to like you, and I thank you for liking me, but I do not like sulky love."

"My love's anyhow honest," said Owen, "and that's more than you can say of...."

"Now shame on you," cried the girl, interrupting him. "Will you say slander of a man behind his back? And to me, too, that know it is slander? And is that the way to change my mind?"

"I have no hopes of that, Mercy," answered the rustic. "And, for your sake, I hope Michael's a better man than I think. Remember the evening under the thorns on the cliff. It is for you and not for me I say it. And methinks you haven't heard much of Michael since he went away to London."

"Then I didn't ask your advice, Mr. Edward," said Mercy, "and you may as well keep it till I do. I dare say I can take care of myself. And very likely Michael has quite plenty to do in London without the writing of letters. And I expect he'll be down here before long, for I hear say that Pendar'l's getting ready for the ladies, if they're not there already. And then you can tell him what you think, like a man. So I wish you a good evening."

"Good evening, Mercy," returned the young man, sadly, and they proceeded on their respective ways.

Ready as the maiden was to defend her lover to another, she could not so easily excuse him to herself. And the anxiety, for the relief of which she had made her pilgrimage to St. Madron's Well, had come back before she reached her mother's cottage at Trevethlan, darkened rather than alleviated by the result of the expedition.

CHAPTER V.

Di, majorum umbris tenuem et sine pondere terram,
Spirantesque crocos, et in urnà perpetuum ver,
Qui præceptorem sancti voluere parentisEsse loco.

Juvenal.

Light lie the earth upon the shades of those,
Flowers deck their graves, Spring dwell with their repose,
Of old who deemed the teacher should supply
The parent's holy rule, heart, hand, and eye.

Meantime Michael Sinson's scheme was ripening into action. The plot matured in the metropolis was about to break on the towers of Trevethlan. Two gentlemen crossed one another in the hurry of Lincoln's Inn, and stopped to exchange a cordial greeting and a little chat.

"By the by, Winter," said Mr. Truby, as they were parting, "we're bringing ejectment against a client of yours."

"Indeed!" exclaimed the second lawyer, "and who may that be?"

"Oh, the parties are old antagonists," answered the first. "It's by no means the first time we've met. Doc d Pendarrel *v.* Trevethlan. Clerk gone down to serve declaration and notice. You'll hear of it in a post or two."

"Good Heaven!" thought Mr. Winter, as he proceeded on his way; "what new calamity is this? Is not that hapless family even yet sufficiently broken? Poor Morton! Now I will wager this comes in some way out of that mad scheme."

And indeed it might well seem that nothing was needed to increase the gloom that invested Trevethlan Castle. It was lonely and desolate in the lifetime of its late possessor, but there was then at least the buoyancy of youth to relieve the dreary monotony; and now, even that had vanished. So far was Helen from being able to restore anything like cheerfulness to her brother, that she herself became infected by his sombre moodiness. Strange was the contrast between those dimly latticed Gothic apartments, and the light and lively saloons of Pendarrel: the wanderer in the former almost dreading to break the silence with his footfall, and the latter ringing with careless laughter and mirthful conversation. Polydore Riches himself could with difficulty preserve his ever-hopeful equanimity; and Griffith often reproached himself to his wife for the facility with which he consented to that ill-omened visit to the metropolis: while the few domestics began to fear moving about singly after dusk, and to whisper of mysterious sounds heard, and sights seen, in the darkening corridors.

Such tales spread outside the castle, and were improved upon in their progress. It became rumoured that the spirit of the unhappy Margaret wandered through its halls in the silence of night, and harassed the children she was not permitted to love in her lifetime. The villagers began to look upon Randolph as the easterns do upon one possessed of the evil eye, and rather shunned than courted his familiarity. And some of the older folk recalled his father's marriage, and began to ask themselves, was it after all only a mockery? Then, indeed, would poor Margaret have cause to seek vengeance for the deceit by which she was beguiled. And so they went on stringing story upon story, until in the rush of the night wind they heard the wailings and howlings which in days long gone were said to portend disaster to the house of Trevethlan.

Randolph was entirely unconscious of the popular mysticism, and too much absorbed in his own feelings to have heeded it in any case. Every day he went forth to the outskirts of the park of Pendarrel, and roamed round its circuit, in the hope of meeting Mildred; and every day that he returned disappointed, made him more restless and reserved. Such an excursion at last led him by Wilderness Gate, and it happened that Maud Basset was sunning herself there as he passed.

"Randolph Trevethlan," she cried, as he went by; and he turned, and she came out to the plot of grass to meet him.

"Randolph Trevethlan," she repeated, "son of a murdered mother, there's a dark hour at hand for thy house, but not darker than is due. I see it written on thy brow. I heard it in the screams that came down on the wind of the night. Say they her spirit is abroad in the towers where her bliss was made her bane? Ay, he is dead, but he shall answer it in his son."

The wildness of the old crone's language suited Randolph's humour. She came quite close to him and looked up in his face.

"Hast seen her?" she asked, lowering her voice to a whisper, "hast seen her, grandson Randolph? Thou knowest who I mean—thy mother, boy. My Margaret, my winsome Margaret. They tell me she's been seen in the castle. 'Tis long, long sin' I saw her myself. They said she grew pale and pale, but they wouldna let me come nigh. And is it true they say? Hast seen her, grandson Randolph?"

"Ay, it is true, indeed," he answered, in a bewildered manner. "I have seen her indeed."

There was the trunk of a large tree lying on the grass close beside them. The old woman took his hand and drew him to a seat upon it. He had neither the power nor the wish to resist.

"Now I can see thee," Maud said. "Thou'st grown so tall; but art not like the gleesome lad that used to sport with my Michael. Woe's me! And how did she look? Said she aught to thee?"

"She hung over my bed with a sweet smiling face, and she bent down and kissed my lips."

"A sweet smiling face!" Maud echoed; "that was hers indeed, my own Margaret. And she smiled on thee, and kissed thee! Then she doth not hate thee?"

"Why should she, Maud?"

"Art thou not his son? and did he not murder her?" exclaimed the crone, in her former harsh manner. "Who said there was no marriage? He! he! Surely thou wilt defend her fame, Randolph Trevethlan?"

"With my life," he answered.

"What's this I'm saying?" again Maud cried, checking herself. "There's a dark hour at hand for thy house, I tell thee. God give thee the strength to bear it!"

And she faltered away as quickly as she could, passed through the gate, and entered the lodge, leaving Randolph still seated, motionless, upon the timber.

Old Maud Basset was deeply versed in all the wild superstitions which still lingered among the Cornubians. She knew the presages which foretold sorrow or death to different old houses. Here, the fall of one of the trees in the avenue was the harbinger of dole; there, ancient logs of timber rose to the surface of the pool in the park before a coming vacancy at the family board. She could tell, too, how drowned persons broke the stillness of night by hailing their own names; of the candle borne by unseen hands in the track of a future funeral; of many a kind of unholy augury; of evil spirits who led wayfarers astray, and precipitated them from the summit of their carns; and in particular of Tregagel, condemned for his many ill deeds to empty the fathomless pool of Dosmary by means of a limpet shell with a hole in it.

The incoherence of the old woman's speech, and her half-uttered predictions, tallied very exactly with some of the feelings which had of late been familiar to Randolph. Mildred, indeed, still occupied by far the greatest portion of them; but his thoughts not unfrequently wandered from her to the dream which had visited him the first night of his return to the castle, and the fair face which had been pressed to his own. That the features so revealed were those of his mother he never doubted, and he felt a restless desire to learn something of the parent whom he had lost before he was three years' old. But to whom should he apply for information? Where could he find the sympathy which such a topic demanded? The long silence that had been observed respecting it, within the castle, must, he thought, have been the effect, in part, of a deficiency of interest, and therefore he was reluctant to open his wishes, even to the chaplain. And without the walls he knew no one to confer with on such a subject. So he was at once fascinated by old Maud's sudden allusion to her child, and answered her questions from the recollections of his dream.

But what did she mean by her reiterated reference to Margaret's death, and her dark announcement of coming calamity? The latter, indeed, harmonized but too well with his own gloomy forebodings—"Who said there was no marriage?—Thou wilt defend her fame?" What was the meaning of such ominous insinuations? Randolph mused on them, without quitting the posture in which Maud had left him, until they became so oppressive, that he resolved to learn all the story from Polydore, without delay.

In the dusk of the evening, he walked with the chaplain in the picture-gallery of the castle. The dim light which came through the high Gothic windows, gave strange and unintended expression to some of the portraits, and left others in such deep shadow that they could hardly be discerned, while the vaulted ceiling hung indistinct over head. Randolph paused at length before the likeness of his father. It was painted when Henry Trevethlan was in the prime of youth, and presented the aspect of a man very different indeed from the cold and stern personage with whom his son was acquainted.

"What changed that countenance, Mr. Riches?" Randolph asked. "What swept away the ardour and enthusiasm which beam from all those lineaments? From what he told me himself, in his dying hour, I framed a tale of hopeless attachment, of love striving to forget itself in ruin. Was it so? Did Esther Pendarrel indeed break my poor father's heart, after trifling with its affection? Methinks, he was not a man to be made a mock of. Yet the mocker has prevailed."

"Randolph," Polydore answered, with a deep sigh, "your speech brings back days of sorrow, which I would were forgotten. But that was all past before I became a resident here. From the steward only, and from popular report, did I learn the intimacy which once subsisted between your father and Mrs. Pendarrel. It was in a thoughtless hour, if all that's said be true, that she crushed his last hopes by wedding. And so, by this time, she knows, perhaps, too well."

"Did she love him, then, Mr. Riches?" Randolph inquired quickly.

"Nay," said the chaplain, "that is a question which I cannot answer. But sure I am, that if one spark of feeling yet lives in her heart, as I would fain believe, she must be visited with deep remorse as often as she looks back upon the ruin wrought by her girlish levity. May you, my dear Randolph, never know the pangs of affection unrequited, or requited only to be broken. And, if such sad lot be yours, may Heaven teach you to bear up against it, nor hide misery in the show of defiance."

"'Tis well for her," Randolph mused aloud, having scarcely heard Polydore's last words, "'tis very well for her, if indeed she loved. For so is no account between us. But if it be otherwise, if, out of wilfulness or vanity, she broke the heart that adored her, then let her look to her own. Not unscathed shall she go down to the grave. Does not the vow lie heavy on my soul?"

"Oh, Randolph, Randolph!" Polydore exclaimed; "what words are these?"

But the young man heeded him not, and, taking his arm, led him several times up and down the long gallery in silence, and at last drew him to one of the windows, from which they looked forth upon the sea. The white crests of the waves were still visible in the increasing darkness.

"Pardon me, Mr. Riches," Randolph said, "if I recall days that are gone, and which are recollected only with pain. But these are topics which have been forbidden, which I can no longer resist approaching, on which I must be informed. My father's marriage, my mother.... How came it about? How did she die? Strange tales have fallen upon my ears——"

The chaplain was much distressed. "What!" thought he, "will they not let poor Margaret rest even in her grave? Do they bear their foul scandal to her son? And is it for me to tell him the story of his father's fault?"

"Speak, Mr. Riches," said Randolph, with some impatience; "let me hear all the truth of the history."

"You know not what you ask," Polydore answered sadly. "Margaret Basset could not resist the influence which made her the seeming mistress of this castle. I could not approve—I went away. The marriage was strictly private. The people were very jealous. Some said—be patient—that it was not duly performed. I know that it was. I had some slight acquaintance with Mr. Ashton the clergyman; he was murdered shortly after the ceremony, and the witness disappeared. The rumours spread; but they died away when you were born. You can imagine the details."

"How did she die?" Randolph asked again.

"You know your father, Randolph," the chaplain replied. "Cannot you conceive the position was too much for her? And her kindred were imprudent. She pined away. But she was an angel. We all loved her. If the devotion of those around her could have made up for the affection which should hallow her situation, surely she were living now."

His hearer mused again for some time in silence, thinking of his dream; and it produced its usual effect of soothing his excitement, and tranquillizing his spirits.

"Come, Mr. Riches," he said, "let us seek my sister. We must not leave her desolate too long."

But the chaplain laid his hand on his old pupil's arm, saying:

"One moment, Randolph; let me detain you one moment. Let me play the master again. What we have been discoursing of will be best forgotten. And oh! let it not be remembered in one fatal sense! Let not these sad events be the foundation of evils yet to come! You spoke of a vow. Such are often wrongly demanded and rashly given. Pride lingers on the bed of death, and bequeaths itself to its successors. Vengeance, unappeased, requires satisfaction by the hands of its heir. So hatred is handed down for ever, and rancour and strife made perpetual. Pray Heaven the vow you speak of requires none of these things! Pray Heaven, that if haply it do, it will be revoked and forgotten!"

"A parent's curse," said Randolph in a hollow voice, "is a terrible thing."

"To him!" the chaplain exclaimed. "To him it is, indeed, a terrible thing, and to his children, if it impels them into wrong-doing. There is no power in man to curse, my dear pupil, and surely Heaven is deaf to all such imprecations."

Alas! Polydore might as well have reasoned with the foaming waves beneath him. Randolph listened in respectful silence, but entirely unconvinced. As law is silent amid the din of arms, so is reason in the conflict of passions. Few sources have been more fruitful of evil than the pledges extorted by the dying. The giver succumbs absolutely to an obligation he ought never to have undertaken, allows himself no discretionary power, yields nothing to the alteration of circumstances, and acts as if the behest were imposed by certain foreknowlege and unerring wisdom. There is no absolution from a death-bed promise, and no chancery to qualify its mischievous engagements.

This conversation was little adapted to restore Polydore Riches to his old equanimity. Gentle and simple-hearted, he was ill-calculated to wrestle with the stormy passions which had desolated his late patron's life, and now threatened shipwreck to the happiness of his pupil. He mourned for the day when, in pride and confidence, neglecting the worldly-wisdom of the more prudent steward, he enthusiastically bade the brother and sister go forth on their way, and foretold for them a prosperous career, and a joyful return. He almost blamed himself for not having given them more adequate preparation for the struggle of life, and attributed their failure to his own deficiency. Yet surely never did teacher better answer the desire of those ancients, lauded by the Roman poet in the lines which head this chapter. Polydore had nothing wherewith to reproach himself.

But the discourse had also revived his own particular griefs, recalling, as it did, the days when he paid his first vows of love to Rose Griffith, and won her timid consent, only to see her wither away. A pensive melancholy was visible upon his countenance when he returned with Randolph through the gloomy galleries to the apartments over the little flower-garden.

CHAPTER VI.

"Guare wheag, yw guare teag."

Cornish Proverb.

"Fair play is good play."

POLWHELE.

Many of the villagers of Trevethlan were desirous of celebrating the return of their young master by some kind of holiday. They remembered how in the old time there were several festivals in the course of the year, kept with high revelry on the green of the hamlet, countenanced by the presence of the lords, and graced by that of the ladies, of its ancient castle. But when ruin fell upon the late possessor, and desolation encompassed his dwelling, the sports diminished in spirit, and the peasantry sought in the neighbouring villages the merriment which no longer enlivened their own. The succession of a young heir, however, seemed to warrant an attempt to revive the much-regretted pastimes, and the idea, when once started, found a staunch supporter in the laughter-loving landlady of the "Trevethlan Arms." Indeed she undertook to roast a sheep, and broach a hogshead of cider, as the foundation of a free feast; and the liberality being met with similar offers from other quarters, the hamlet was in a position to offer tolerably profuse hospitality to all comers.

Valentine's day was fixed upon for the revel; and several evenings before it came, some of the villagers met at Dame Miniver's, to arrange the programme of the sports. And it was finally decided to revive the old game of hurling, by challenging Pendarrel to play them home and home across the country, as the principal event of the frolic. The determination, however, was not unopposed.

"Are ye sure, neighbours," said our acquaintance Germoe, the tailor, "that this challenge will be agreeable on the hill? Ye know what we spoke of only the other night. There's no love lost between the hall and the castle."

"The very cause for why to play out the quarrel," said Edward Owen. "And as to the castle, I warrant the young squire'll be none displeased to hear we've given Pendar'l a beating. I say play."

"But in such case," urged farmer Colan, "playing often turns to fighting."

"And what then?" Owen asked again, who took great interest in the meditated match, from a vague hope of encountering his rival in the hostile ranks,—"what then, I say? Have we not thrashed them before? 'Tis ill nursing a quarrel."

"Ay, ay, lad," said Mrs. Miniver aside to the last speaker, "I know where thy cap's set. She's a proud minx, and an' I were thee———. But, neighbours, how long has Trevethlan been afraid of Pendar'l?"

A true woman's question, and one which settled the matter off-hand. There was no further hesitation as to despatching the challenge. The tailor's hint concerning the castle had, however, more foundation than was supposed; for Randolph much regretted the resolution of his dependents. But he did not learn it until the invitation had been sent and accepted, and it was then impossible to retreat.

On the other side, the match received the formal sanction of Mrs. Pendarrel, who had been at the park a day or two when the proposal arrived. Remembering that her retainers far outnumbered those of Trevethlan, she rather rejoiced at the prospect of humiliating her adversary, and graciously promised to provide the silver-plated ball with which the game should be played.

The village green was "home" for the players of Trevethlan. Early in the appointed holiday it was thronged with busy, noisy groups, and presented an extremely lively aspect, strikingly at variance with its recent tranquillity, and with the sombre gravity of the castle, where there were no symptoms of participation in the frolics of the day. Reverend elders occupied the bench round the old chestnut in front of the inn, and discoursed of the matches of their youth, before the harmony of Trevethlan and Pendarrel was interrupted, and when the open doors of the castle proffered unbounded hospitality. Stalwart youths, girded for the sport, strolled about in knots, plotting devices for carrying off the ball, arranging plans for watching the enemy's home, cracking jests with the maidens who idled in the throng, in their Sunday frocks and smartest ribbands, and extorting half promises of reward in the evening for prowess displayed in the day. Dame Miniver had ample cause for satisfaction with the result of her liberality.

Mrs. Pendarrel permitted her side to make the lawn before her house their home. Refreshments of all kinds were distributed among the crowd there collected with a bounteous hand. The lady herself descended among her tenants, leaning on the arm of her daughter, speaking to old acquaintance, everywhere bestowing encouragement. Even Mildred was excited by the liveliness of the scene. It was a fine genial day, with a warm breeze blowing, which kept the trees in constant motion, and gave life to the company beneath their leafless branches.

Michael Sinson, only just arrived from London, was to lead the forces of Pendarrel. So his patroness, aware of his former reputation, desired; so his vanity, as well as his duty, prompted. He was active in the throng, assigning their stations to his mates, providing for all the chances of the struggle, but glancing ever and anon on the fair young form that glided through the rustic assembly like a being from another sphere. Little thought he that morning of the rosy-cheeked girl whom he had once pretended to love, and who now walked among the maidens of Trevethlan, with a sympathy divided between her sweetheart and her home.

The goals were not much more than two miles apart, a short distance in a match "to the country;" but this circumstance prevented the interference of horsemen, diminished the opportunities for artifice, and made the contest depend more on the personal skill and prowess of the players. In a longer game the ball might be thrown into the hands of a mounted partizan, who would trust to the speed of his horse to carry it home in triumph; or again into the keeping of a rustic, selected for his simple appearance, who would trudge tranquilly along the high road seemingly unconscious of his valuable charge, while the hurlers on both sides sought the prize with great animation; until the news of the crafty bearer's arrival at his destination told the victory of his friends, and both parties repaired to the winning quarters to laugh over the trick, and fight the battle anew, in a high jollification.

There was a meadow situated on an eminence about midway between Trevethlan and Pendarrel, between which and either goal no obstacle intervened to turn aside the play. Here it was arranged the ball should be thrown up, and hither Mrs. Pendarrel and Mildred repaired to behold the commencement of the game. The players chosen to begin stood in an irregular ring on the hill, and amongst them Sinson and Owen, the opposing generals, the latter of whom regarded the former with looks which indicated more ill-will than befitted the occasion, but which Michael observed with contemptuous indifference.

And now Mildred has tossed the new apple of discord, a wooden ball, some three inches in diameter, covered with silver, and bearing the motto which heads this chapter, as the trophy, to remain in the possession of the victors of the day, into the middle of the ring, and a dozen men are on the ground, struggling to obtain a hold of the prize. Rolling over and over, twisting, tangled like a coil of snakes, they writhe and struggle in intricate confusion. Where is the ball? Who shall discern it in so close a conflict? See, a combatant shakes himself clear of competitors, rises in the midst, springs over them, and bounds away in the direction of Pendarrel, cheered by the partizans of the hall. Not long shall the cheering endure: an opponent bars his career: him the holder of the ball thrusts aside, "butts" with his closed fist. Reprisal in like fashion is against the rules. But there is another, and another, one at a time, for so it is ordained. Nor are the holder's friends inactive: they screen him round, and strive to keep off his adversaries. And thus he makes some way, but may not even clear the field. His vigour fails at last under repeated attacks; he has no longer strength to butt; "hold," he must cry, in token of surrender, and deal the ball to be seized by fresher hands: a stouter heart, he thinks, 't were hard to find.

Again the first struggle is renewed, but the crowd is not so great, nor does it last so long. This time the ball is borne swiftly back in the direction of Trevethlan. Light of foot is the holder, but his speed shall not avail him long. At the very hedge of the field he is encountered; he may not pass the barrier; he tries another point, again to be defeated; he, too, must shout the word of submission, and recover breath for a renewed onset.

And thus, with varied fortune, the game proceeds, continually growing wider in its scene. The ball is borne in succession towards either goal, far away from the field where the game began. It seems the lady of Pendarrel reckoned without her host, for there are many volunteers in the play, and they, with proper heroism, have chosen the weaker side. She and her daughter have retired to the hall, but the country is still alive with the excitement of the game, and the woods and the sky are vocal with the cries of the rival partizans, as they mark the course of the ball with shouts of "Ware east," "Ware west."

An old writer compares the ball used in this game to an evil demon; for, says he, no sooner does a player become possessed of it than he acts as if he were possessed of a devil; flying like a madman over the country, bursting through hedges, bounding over ditches, rushing furiously against all opponents, heedless of everything but his progress towards home. When suddenly, having been obliged at last to surrender, he becomes once more tranquil and peaceable, as though the evil spirit had then left him, and entered his successor, who instantly commences a like impetuous career.

Many a possession of this kind was witnessed in the match between Pendarrel and Trevethlan. Once the former hamlet seemed almost on the point of victory. The holder had disencumbered himself of all who had been active in the field, and was dashing triumphantly homewards, when he met the reserve especially stationed to prevent a surprise. At the same moment Owen bounded up to rally his forces. The game was rescued, and renewed with increased vigour on both hands. Step by step the path of the holder, now on this side and now on that, was contested in every way permitted by the laws of the game. Passion grew hotter, and ever and anon rose cries of "foul." The leaders, who had hitherto rather directed the fray than engaged in it personally, now rushed into the thick of the fight. The partizans of Trevethlan gained ground in their turn. The chestnut on their green was already in sight. Owen himself held the ball. The road, for the fight had descended from the fields into the highway, was thronged with the combatants. The maidens of the village, approached the end of the green, and joined in the animating cries. Owen had repelled many an antagonist, when Michael Sinson met him face to face. It was what he had long wished for, and he was delighted when, as he always affirmed and as was sturdily maintained by all his partizans, his opponent butted him unfairly. The excitement of the game and personal exasperation united to give force to the blow which sent his rival staggering away. The next moment Owen stood on the grass of the hamlet, and flung the ball high into the air, while loud and reiterated shouts proclaimed the victory of Trevethlan, and were heard, perhaps not without some satisfaction, within the walls of the castle.

Whatever ill-blood might have been generated in the heat of the engagement, rapidly subsided when it was over. It had been gallantly fought, and discomfiture was only less honourable than success. Victor and vanquished met in friendly groups on the green, formed parties for the athletic sports of the country, or sought partners for the dance which would terminate the amusements of the day, while the landlady of the Trevethlan Arms was finishing her preparations for the feast, and the children were continually increasing a pile of combustibles in front of the inn, destined to blaze after nightfall in celebration of the holiday.

There was, however, one breast in which disappointed rage still rankled. Michael Sinson rose after the fall he received from Owen, to hear the acclamations hailing his conqueror, and to feel an aggravation of his animosity, not so much against his rival, as against Trevethlan, its master, and its inhabitants. He looked angrily at the jocund doings on the green, and then turned to bear the tidings of his defeat to his patroness. But he had not proceeded many steps, when a light hand was laid upon his arm, and a sharp glance round showed him the rosy cheeks and black eyes of Mercy Page.

"Why, Michael," said the maiden, "is this the welcome ye learn to give in London? Is this the way ye would leave Mercy to seek for a partner at a village revel? What if we have won the match, is it a cause for shame?"

"Pish!" Sinson said, sulkily. "Go to your Edward Owen. He is the hero of the day. Let him be your partner."

"Then it's not heroes, nor none such I care for," pursued the wilful girl. "I'm no sure I'm glad that our side's won. Come now, Michael, what's to fret for?"

Sinson cast his sinister eyes upon Mercy's face. It was very pretty, even in reproach, and besides, he thought she might be of use to him.

"May-be," said he, "I shall be back in the evening. But now I must take the news to Pendarrel."

With which ungracious saying, Mercy was forced to content herself, and return, pouting, to her mirthful companions, while Michael pursued his way to Wilderness Lodge.

His old grandmother asked him concerning the game, and on being surlily informed of its result, muttered something about a judgment on such sacrilegious doings, which her dutiful grandson did not hear, and if he had, would have laughed at. His patroness learned the news with an air of indifference, which to him appeared at variance with her previous interest in the match; and as he left her presence, he could not help saying, that Trevethlan should yet pay dearly for the morning's victory.

Meantime the feast was spread in a low, long barn at the Trevethlan Arms, and the board was crowded by adherents of both parties with right west-country appetites. Lads and lasses ate to their heart's content. Dame Miniver's sheep was declared to make very excellent mutton, and no one quarrelled with the quality of her cider. The guests from Pendarrel honoured the health of the squire of Trevethlan, and the company who were at home paid due respect to the lord and lady of the strangers. So "all went merry as a marriage bell." The relics of dinner were reserved to furnish forth a supper, and the company resumed their morning sports, exhilarating themselves with copious libations of the juice of the apple, and occasionally with a dram of whisky or Hollands, which was, probably, still indebted to his Majesty's customs.

On the whole, the frolic proceeded in perfect good-humour; but occasionally a dispute arose respecting the final contest between Owen and Sinson, which threatened for a moment or more to interrupt the general harmony. No serious quarrel had arisen, however, before daylight died away, and the shadow of night called for the lighting of the bonfire. But when the crackling logs flung a ruddy glow over the green, and the white smoke went circling away on the breeze, and the village musicians, a fiddle and clarionet, who on Sunday led the choir in church, became more energetic in their strains, then the fun began to grow fast and furious, and practical jokes continually endangered the peace of the green. As the boys and girls danced wild country measures around the blazing pile, a few of their comrades distributed at each end of a long and stout cord, would single a couple from the throng, catch them in the snare, and running adroitly round and round in opposite directions, bind the unlucky pair in a noose to which they would not have objected, perhaps, in a gentler and quieter assembly, but which here exposed them to many a shout of rustic laughter. Or, again, running rapidly along the green with the cord trailing loose between them, the same confederates would trip up the heels of all in their way—a jest not always accepted with perfect equanimity.

In the midst of these rough gambols, and when no small portion of the folks had somewhat exceeded the bounds of sobriety, Michael Sinson made his appearance on the green, himself flushed with festive doings at Pendarrel. He spoke and laughed with some of his acquaintance, and sought his neglected flame, Mercy Page. She sat on a stool at her mother's cottage-gate, having steadily refused every invitation to take an active part in the dance, relying on the half-promise she had received from Michael. As for her rejected lover, the hero of the day, he seemed to challenge her jealousy by dancing vigorously with half the girls on the green, and ostentatiously parading his partners in Mercy's sight; without, however, succeeding in his object, by awaking her indignation.

Sinson soon discovered his too faithful beauty, and led her, willing enough, for a romping dance around the bonfire. But they had tripped together for a very short time, when the rope was swept round them, and in a twinkling they were fast enveloped in its coils. Michael grew furious with rage. He recollected having once boasted to Mercy of rescuing her from a similar disaster. His wrath was far from diminished when he perceived Owen active in endeavouring to procure his release. When those efforts succeeded, he fixed a quarrel upon his rescuer, on the old ground of the foul play at the hurling-match. Mischief was meant, and mischief came. In a very few minutes the whole green was the scene of a furious conflict; the parties which had met in the morning in friendly rivalry, and broken bread together cheerfully in the afternoon, now proceeding to break one another's heads without the slightest reserve. The girls ran crying to their homes; the bonfire was trodden under foot; and so, in confusion and uproar, terminated the sports at Trevethlan.

The battle might be considered in its end as drawn. But it was said that individual cries were heard in the fray, to the effect that the heir of the castle was about to claim his own, and that they would have tidings of him at Pendarrel before many weeks had gone by. If the bonfire at Trevethlan was extinguished in tumult, some of the hamlet would dance by the light of a greater. No one seemed to know what such words meant, but some folks remembered them when the heat of the struggle was past.

CHAPTER VII.

"Whether it be
Bestial oblivion, or some craven scruple
Of thinking too precisely on the event—
A thought, which, quartered, hath but one part wisdom,
And ever three parts coward—I do not know
Why yet I live to say, *This thing 's to do*."

SHAKSPEARE.

Randolph had not renewed, on returning to the castle, the instructions he formerly gave to Jeffrey respecting the non-admission of strangers. But as yet there had been no visitors. The family had been so long isolated, that it was a matter of discussion among the neighbouring gentry to call or not to call; and no sheep had as yet chosen to head the flock. But the very morning of the sports described in the last chapter, word was brought that a gentleman wished to see Mr. Trevethlan. Randolph desired he might be shown into a parlour, and went to meet him.

"Have the honour to address Mr. Trevethlan, I presume," the stranger said. "My name, Stiles; in the employment of Messrs. Truby and Company, solicitors, Chancery-lane, London. Have the honour to deliver this declaration in ejectment. Will take the liberty to read the notice—'Mr. Randolph Trevethlan'"———

"It is unnecessary, sir," said Randolph, with an external calmness at which he afterwards marvelled. "I have been a student of the law, and understand the proceeding."

"Beg pardon, sir," said Mr. Stiles; "more regular to read it. Very short. 'Mr. Randolph Trevethlan'"———

And the clerk read the notice without further interruption. Randolph took the paper, rang the bell, desired the servant to provide Mr. Stiles with some refreshment, wished him good-morning, and withdrew.

He was, as he said, perfectly familiar with the nature of the law-suit which this visit commenced. And as the reader is doubtless acquainted with it through the medium of a very clever and popular story, it will be unnecessary to pursue its details here. As soon as Randolph was alone, he glanced down the document, and, with a kind of wild glee, perceived that his real opponent in the action was Philip Trevethlan Pendarrel. He rubbed his hands together, rumpling the paper between them, and almost exulting in the strife which was at hand.

"So," said he aloud, "there are two games begun to-day. One will be played out before night; the other will last sometime longer. But we'll make it as short as we can. And now to action. Our stake is a little higher than that of the villagers yonder. They play for broken heads, and we for broken hearts. Faites vos devoirs, preux chevaliers."

With these hasty words Randolph immediately sought the chaplain and steward, and begged them to come and assist at a council of war. Nor was Helen omitted, for after one moment's hesitation, her brother thought she had better know the worst at once. As soon as the little circle was completed, Randolph produced the hostile missive, requested that he might not be interrupted, and read it from end to end with a fierce gravity of accent. Helen was entirely bewildered, Polydore was rather perplexed, the steward was thunderstruck.

"What does it mean?" said Helen. "Roe, and Doe, and Mr. Pendarrel! What does it all mean?"

"It is some kind of law proceeding, is it not?" said the chaplain.

"It is the beginning of an action of ejectment," said Mr. Griffith. "That is, Mr. Pendarrel claims some portion of our estates. Methinks he has had enough already."

Randolph was silent.

"I imagined that all litigation had been closed long ago," Polydore remarked.

"Will it be a source of trouble?" Helen asked, looking anxiously at her brother.

"I cannot for the life of me understand what it means," said Griffith, who had been reflecting. "Is it possible that in all those numerous deeds, some bit of land has been included which has never been surrendered? But it cannot be—they're too sharp."

"Trouble yourself with no vain questions, Mr. Griffith," Randolph exclaimed abruptly. "This is brought for the castle, and hamlet, and *all* our property."

"To deprive us——," Helen began.

"Ay, Helen, to deprive us of everything," her brother continued. "Some personal trinkets, a few bits of old furniture, perhaps our wardrobes, may be spared—that is, if we can pay the expenses of the proceeding. But our home, and our lands, and our friends, from all those we are to be parted for ever."

Helen wept; more at her brother's manner than the fate announced in his words.

"Randolph," said the chaplain, with a sternness, which in him was extremely rare, "be calm. You are unkind to your sister, and unjust to us. You know that nothing but your own conduct can deprive you of your friends, and I apprehend that even the rest does not necessarily follow."

"Sister, dearest," Randolph whispered, "I did not mean it. Mr. Riches, I beg pardon. I am, perhaps, scarcely myself. But I feel convinced that nothing less is intended than an attack on the castle. It is well to provide against the worst."

"I think Mr. Trevethlan must be right," said the steward very seriously. "On turning the matter over, I can see no other explanation than an attempt to upset our title in general. But what can be the alleged flaw I am wholly at a loss to conceive."

"One cannot learn that till the trial, Mr. Griffith," Randolph observed.

"And is it possible," asked Helen, who had dried her eyes, "that the attempt can be successful? Can we be obliged to abandon Trevethlan?"

"Not for ever, my sister," answered Randolph. "The word slipped from my tongue. But they may obtain a temporary victory. We may be surprised at the first trial. It is for that I wished to prepare you. It is also a reason why I am resolved the affair shall, on our side, be hurried forward as fast as possible. We will try at the very next assizes, if it is feasible, and so, within a month, we shall know our true position. I shall write to Mr. Winter, and send him this notice immediately; and Mr. Griffith will have the goodness to communicate with him also. Say everything you can imagine, my good sir. Suggest the wildest difficulties. Perhaps Mr. Riches can think of something. We will be forearmed if we can. But despatch—despatch above everything."

Randolph had recovered both his composure and his energy. Riches and Griffith were again surprised at the decision with which he spoke. They now quitted the room, and the brother and sister were left alone.

"Helen," the former said, "this may be a very painful business. From the nature of the proceeding, we are kept in ignorance of the grounds of the attack, and when they are disclosed we may be taken by surprise, and unable to show their weakness. And in that case there would be a verdict against us, and for a time—note me, my dear sister, only for a time—we should be deprived of everything that is ours, to our very name. So, Helen, we must be prepared for a season of calamity."

"They cannot deprive me of you, Randolph," she said, "and the rest they may take."

"Nay," said the brother, "I hope they may not. There is some deep plot laid against us, which may prove successful at first. Dark hints, foreboding threats, have been whispered to me. I seem to see some shapeless danger. It is now like the smoke which rose from the fisherman's casket. It may take the form of the Afrite. But trust me, my sister, we shall find a spell to charm it again into its prison."

"Would, Randolph," Helen exclaimed, "I could find some spell to charm you into old ways! Why are you not as before we went to London? Whence has come all the change? Little else should I heed, if you were as you used to be."

"And all the glories of our race! Fie, Helen! Go to Mrs. Griffith, and take a lesson in the picture-gallery."

He had smiled as he began; but his last word suggested a host of recent associations, and his tone was gloomy again, as he said he would go and write his letters.

Of these, the first was to Mr. Winter. Randolph referred him to the document which he enclosed, requested him to communicate with Messrs. Truby, and to take upon himself the whole conduct of the action. And, in the most urgent terms, he desired the lawyer to bring it to an issue with the utmost despatch. Some surprise, he said, was evidently intended. It was just within the sphere of possibility, that by delay they might find a clue to the plot. Never mind that. It was at least as possible they might not, and they might as well learn it from their adversaries. Beaten at first, they would triumph in the end. At the same time, they would of course go into court prepared, as far as they could be, to meet every possible objection that could be imagined. He would be obliged by Mr. Winter retaining Mr. Seymour Rereworth as his junior counsel.

Randolph had signed his letter, and laid down his pen. He read carefully over what he had written, caught up the quill again, and added—

"P.S.—It is my father's marriage that is attacked."

With quick and trembling fingers he folded the missive, sealed and directed it. So much was done.

Then he wrote to Rereworth, who had been called to the bar the preceding term, and intended to join the western circuit at the coming assizes. The letter was as follows:—

> "MY DEAR REREWORTH,
>
> "An action has just been commenced against me, in which I have requested Winter to offer you a brief. If you will not object to hold it, I shall rejoice; but if, under the

circumstances, you feel the slightest reluctance, pray decline without hesitation. Do not think that a refusal would vex me.

"It is ejectment, brought by Mr. Pendarrel, and, I have no doubt, for all the property which is left me here. There can be only three grounds for the claim. First, they may set up some will or deed, which would be forged. Secondly, they may impeach the marriage of my grandfather (Mr. Pendarrel's half brother), which is very unlikely. Thirdly, they may attack my father's; which, I write it with shame and sorrow, is what I believe they mean to do.

"Winter is acquainted with all the circumstances of that unhappy union. I have written to him; but I could not dwell upon the subject. To you I would hint, that it is among my maternal relations that a clue to the plot will probably be found. They have, perhaps, had reason to complain, and they have passion enough to seek revenge.

"I levy a tax upon your friendship in asking you to engage in a cause which, you will at once see, involves many personal considerations, and must produce great pain. Do not, I again say, consider yourself in any way bound to pay it; and believe me, whatever be your decision, to be, my dear Rereworth,

"Still faithfully yours,

"RANDOLPH TREVETHLAN."

These letters, together with one from Mr. Griffith, were despatched to their destination that afternoon. Griffith wrote at much greater length than his master, refreshing Mr. Winter's memory as to many points in the family history. In particular, he detailed all the facts relating to the marriage of Margaret Basset. For it was impossible not to be struck by the idea that this action might be an attempt to give effect to the vulgar rumours. And Griffith remembered, with some anxiety, that the only witness to the ceremony, at present available, was old Maud Basset, and that it was not quite certain which way her testimony might incline. On the other hand, the steward found pleasure in thinking that they could raise so strong a presumption in favour of the marriage, from Mr. Trevethlan's own conduct, and from the conviction of all his household, as could only be shaken by evidence of the most peremptory description.

The temporary excitement which had strung Randolph's nerves and restored his composure while he wrote his letters, died away when they were finished.

The sport with which all the country was alive, precluded him from his usual excursion. He ascended with Helen to the roof of the watch-tower, which commanded a very extensive view of the scene of action, and looked listlessly upon the animated landscape. The shouts of the contending parties came up to the brother and sister, now near and now distant, now from the hollow of a dell, now from the ridge of an upland. Sometimes the holder of the ball led the conflict full in their sight; sometimes it disappeared in the intricacy of a thicket; sometimes it approached, and Trevethlan seemed to be winning; then it receded, and victory appeared to favour Pendarrel. Immediately below them, at the foot of the base-court was the village-green, gay with the bright ribands and merry laughter of the country girls. Helen partly forgot the cares of the new law-suit, in gazing on the jocund landscape.

"I wonder, Randolph," she said, "whether Mercy Page's sweetheart is in the game to-day. The poor little girl's been quite fretting about him, ever since he went away to London; and she owned to me, the other day, she had been to drop a pebble in Madron Well, and that wretched dame Gudhan frightened her half out of her wits."

"Who is Mercy's sweetheart?" her brother asked.

"Oh, it is Michael Sinson. He is in the service of Mrs. Pendarrel." Helen had answered before she recollected the morning's communication.

"Ha! indeed!" Randolph exclaimed.

"And Polydore tells me that Edward Owen is just as peevish for her sake," the sister continued, "as she for her absent swain's. And he goes much among the discontented, and attends the night meetings, all out of love. So you see there's quite a little romance in the hamlet; Romeo and Juliet *en paysan*."

"Of old," Randolph said, mechanically, for his thoughts were otherwise engaged, "he would have gone on the high road."

Helen, perplexed, looked in her brother's face, and saw the abstraction in which he was absorbed. She turned her attention on the game, which was now approaching its close. A dense throng appeared in the lane which debouched at the further end of the green, shouting, struggling, and fighting, till at last the victor of the day bounded to the goal, and threw up the ball in triumph. The acclamations which hailed his success roused Randolph from his reverie.

"See, brother," said Helen, "we have won. Let it be an omen for us."

"Ah!" he replied, smiling fondly upon her, and reverting to an idea she had suggested, "I wish we believed such things. I would consult St. Madron myself. As it is, I have written to consult our friend Rereworth. But the game is over: let us go down."

Helen was pleased to hear that Randolph was in correspondence with one whom she had liked in his visits to Hampstead, and also at the expression of his face, and the cheerful accent with which he spoke. But it was only one of the fluctuations of the barometer in a storm.

He had exulted at first receiving the notice of action, because it gave him what he had wished for,—a personal quarrel with the Pendarrels. Before it he never felt quite satisfied with himself. He had his misgivings concerning his reception of that first letter of condolence. He desired a right to make reprisals on his own account. Anything that would render his union with Esther's daughter a greater triumph over herself, was acceptable to his perverse temper.

But this froward feeling was short-lived. Randolph remembered Mildred's position, and reflected that if she loved him, as he believed, everything that widened the breach between him and her family would be a source of misery to herself. In the pursuit of his selfish revenge, he had entirely forgotten the suffering it would inflict upon his mistress. He was precluded from seeking her as the friend of those who should be dear to her; and it was not, surely, for him to exult in any exasperation of their hostility.

And then he thought of the law-suit almost in despair. It seemed that Esther Pendarrel, not content with breaking his father's heart, and driving him to ruin, was proceeding after his death to defame his memory: pretending that, he had imposed upon his family by a fictitious marriage: seeking to have his children stripped of their name, and made infamous in the eyes of the world. The mother of her whom Randolph loved, was trying to degrade him to a position in which his alliance would be a disgrace.

And his own mother, whom he only knew by that strange dream, yet regarded with the fondest affection, whose fame he had but recently declared he would defend with his life,—her good name was also to be sacrificed to satisfy the vengeance of this haughty woman. What! were these the things in which he had exulted? That the breach which his father had provided one means—dubious and remote indeed, but still a means of healing—should be rendered irremediable for ever! For who could pardon an attack like this?

Of the action itself, and its consequences, Randolph took little heed. To think of it would only be to perplex himself concerning the precise artifice which was to be used at the trial: he was content to wait till it came. Nevertheless, he noted Helen's chance information respecting Michael Sinson's employment, but Griffith had already mentioned it to Mr. Winter.

Late in the evening the steward brought an account of the fray which terminated the village sports, to the little turret-room where Polydore was sitting with his old pupils. Jeffrey had been down on the green, participating in the evening revels; but the careful warder returned to his post as soon as anger took the place of amusement. And so fitful was Randolph's mood that he now heard even of this disturbance with regret, as he fancied it might introduce some fresh element of discord into the family feud.

CHAPTER VIII.

"Era già l'ora che volge 'l disio
A' naviganti, e'ntenerisce il cuore,
Lo di ch'han detto a' dolci amici addio,
E che lo nuovo peregrin d' amore
Punge, se ode squilla di lontano,
Che paja 'l giorno pianger che si muore."

DANTE.

Mercy Page was an old acquaintance of Helen's, and was wont to bring her all the gossip of the village, intermingled with her own little adventures. And so she told Miss Helen the story of her pilgrimage to Madron Well, and the fierce denunciations of Dame Gudhan. And the young lady, after smilingly chiding her for her simple proceeding, taught her to smile also at the ill words of the pythoness. But now Mercy thought she had the laugh on her side, for she had heard the twilight tales about the castle, and availed herself of the familiarity which Helen allowed her, to inquire concerning them at head-quarters.

"D' ye know, Miss Helen," she asked, "what they're saying about the green yonder? How there's a pale lady all in white, that walks through the castle by night, and fleers you and Mr. Randolph sadly?"

"All I can say, Mercy," Helen answered, with a smile, "is that I have met no lady answering that description, either by night or by day."

"They tell it so in whispers," the fair rustic continued; "I cannot well say what is the story. It's something about somebody that some one murdered a very long while ago."

"Ah, Mercy, people are always fond of a ghost story," Helen said. "And so I hear Michael was in the game the other day. You had a merry dance at last, I expect."

"Then, Miss Helen," said the girl, "I don't well know what's come over Michael. He's very different from before he went to London."

Helen sighed, thinking Michael was not the only one who had been so altered. And in truth, Mercy was quite right. If her old lover pretended to court her now, it was in a spirit very opposite to that which animated him before his employment by Mrs. Pendarrel. His object was twofold; to make use of the unsuspecting maiden as a spy within the castle, and to achieve one of those conquests which he had heard boasted of as great exploits in the society he frequented in town. But love is frequently as blind to the qualities of its object as the attachment of animals, and Mercy was as ignorant of Michael's intentions, as the faithful dog in the story, that his master was a murderer.

In truth, Sinson was exceedingly anxious to know what was passing in Trevethlan Castle. He felt a feverish curiosity to discover what was there thought of the law-suit which was just commenced. Certain himself, that the case which he had submitted to Mr. Truby was unassailable, he was still nervously desirous to learn in what manner his opponents prepared to resist it. What did they guess? What did they suspect? What line of investigation did they pursue? The proceedings were like a duel in the dark. Neither party knew anything of his adversary's moves. A stab in the back was perfectly legitimate. And so Sinson, naturally imputing to others the conduct from which he would not shrink himself, trembled lest he might be over-reached after all, and find his artifices recoil upon their deviser.

And upon this cast he had set all his desires. Upon the result of this trial depended the issue of all his weary manœuvring. It would either place him in a position to demand his own terms, or it would leave him unable to obtain any. His victory would be complete, or his ruin total. But so far, although he was eager for news of his opponents, he entertained no doubt whatsoever of his own triumph.

Meantime, he trusted chiefly to Mercy for intelligence of what passed at the castle, and she told him all she knew, with the most innocent frankness. Trembling at shadows, he had been really alarmed at the tale of poor Margaret's apparition. Aware of what was in contemplation, and like all his race prone to superstition, he did not conceive there was anything so very improbable in such a visitation, and he felt that it would not be for the orphans that its warning was intended. He was glad to hear from Mercy that the story was unfounded.

Sinson was also much perturbed by the conduct of his grandmother. She had not forgotten the hint he threw out respecting her favourite's marriage. It was true, she only referred to it to excuse what he had said, but the wild language and fierce predictions in which she indulged, continually troubled him. And, besides, she was the only witness now to be found who was present at the wedding; and although her opposition could in no degree frustrate his scheme, her concurrence would have gone some way to promote it.

But he now endeavoured to hug himself in his security, and to pass the interval before the trial as tranquilly as he might. He chose for himself a pleasanter pastime than espionage upon Trevethlan Castle, and watched with unwearying diligence the steps of Miss Pendarrel. Little did Mildred think, as she pursued her meditative way among the unfrequented thickets of the park, or strolled through the fields and lanes beyond it, or wandered along the cliffs of the sea-shore, that her path was always dogged by the stealthy foot, and her form watched by the sinister eyes of Michael Sinson. Always at a convenient distance, ready to slip behind a tree, or to skulk under a bank, if she chanced accidentally to turn her head, the crafty observer lurked around her course. Many a time he set out with the intention of coming forth at some sequestered spot, and accosting the object of his chase, but he always let the opportunity slip by. A kind of awe fettered his limbs, and restrained his tongue, when he would have advanced and addressed the unsuspecting maiden. There was a proud security about her which he felt it impossible to invade, a serene confidence which he dared not ruffle. He hated his timidity; he said, it should not be so next time; and when the next time came, he again deferred his intended appearance.

It happened, one fine mild afternoon, that Mildred quitted the park by Wilderness Gate, and bent her steps to that thorn-shaded portion of the cliff which was the scene of Michael's interview with Mercy Page, immediately before his first departure for the metropolis. Here she paced backwards and forwards, amongst the leafless hawthorns, often pausing to gaze over the sea, and musing rather sadly of her forlorn situation at home, where she had no one to confide in, no one to share her emotion, and where every day seemed to draw her nearer to a precipice, which she was yet resolved to shun. Thus she was looking over the water, whose transparency assumed the hue of the weeds growing at the bottom, pink, blue, and green, and watching the vessels in the bay, when a step sounded on the turf by her side, and she looked round, and recognised her cousin, Randolph Trevethlan.

"Mildred," he said, in a voice which trembled with excitement, "do you know me, Mildred?"

He might read the answer in the hot flush upon her cheeks and forehead.

"Will you acknowledge the impostor who sought you in disguise?" he continued rapidly; "will you remember him who was shamed in your sight? Me, the avowed enemy of your house, who should have met any belonging to it in defiance and hate, yet came masked to your side to seek an interest in your heart? For it was so. I loved you deeply, devotedly I loved you, before that evening. So I love you now, and shall love you for ever. From the first time my eyes met yours, in that echoing scene of music and of light, I loved you, fervently as when I moved by your side in those glittering saloons, fervently as I do now, and shall do, till my heart has ceased to beat. And it was for me, Randolph Trevethlan, to creep covertly to your presence, and woo you—for I did woo you—woo you to be mine! And will you remember me now? Will you hear me—not seek to palliate a deception which I loathe, not ask for forgiveness which I despise—but will you hear me lay my love at your feet, and, oh Mildred! at least not trample on it?"

The vehemence with which he had spoken at first softened into tenderness in his last words. Mildred continued to walk slowly by his side, unable to speak, scarcely knowing what she did, with her eyes bent down, and her hands clasped before her.

"Hear me," Randolph said, in tones of passionate supplication. "Do you know the life I have led? In yon lone castle by the sea, isolated from the world, ignorant of my race, with nothing to love? Yet discontented, pining, dreaming of love? Do you know how I came forth, madly enthusiastic, to seek for fortune and fame? How still I felt my desolation? Was not the world a blank to me? Was I not alone? Yet how should you know it? I knew it not myself. Not till my eyes met yours knew I the yearnings of my heart. The truth flashed upon me in an instant. To see you and to love you, in your love to find the key to my life, to vow for you to live and die—it was a moment's work. I knew not who you were. Did I heed that? What acquaintance is needed for love? Alas! I knew you too soon. The daughter of my father's destroyer, the child of her whom I was pledged to hate, she it was I was destined to love."

Mildred cast an imploring glance into his face.

"It is vain," he said. "It is hopeless. Even now, at this very hour, she seeks to drive me from my home: from my name: my sister and me to be outcasts on earth: shunned and despised: children without a father. Think you there can be anything but hate between her and me?"

"My mother," Mildred faltered.

"It is our curse," said Randolph. "Did not my father imprecate the wrath of Heaven upon me, if I held communion with her or hers? I love you, Mildred, and the curse has fallen. And you love me," he cried in wild rapture, flinging his arm around her, and folding her to his side, "you love me, let the curse prevail."

She did not shrink from his embrace, and for some distance they proceeded in silence. He pressed her to a seat on a bank of turf.

"Speak, dearest," he whispered, "let me hear that you love me. I feel it in the beating of your heart. I read it in your face. Will you not let me hear it from your lips?"

She hid her face against his breast. There was another long silence.

"Dearest," at length Randolph murmured, "there can be little of joy for our love except in itself. Shall we not have faith in each other to support us? Will you not be mine, whatever betide,—will you not be mine, dearest Mildred?"

"I am yours, Randolph," she said, "yours for ever, and only yours."

He pressed a kiss upon her lips.

"I must go home," she whispered, "I must go home."

"Yes, we must part," the lover answered; "I know it. See," he continued, "it is my star. Smiling on us, Mildred, as that evening. Believe me, dearest, we shall not be parted for ever."

And in a calmer mood, with more of hope and less of agitation, Randolph rose, and supporting Mildred on his arm, accompanied her a short distance on her way. They parted with a silent pressure of hands.

The lovers were scarcely out of sight when Michael Sinson emerged from a lair he had made himself near the spot where they rested, glared fiercely in the direction they had gone, and advanced to the edge of the cliff. The evening was mild enough for May; twilight was stealing slowly over the tranquil sea; in the west, the star of love, alone in the sky, was following the sun to sink behind the waves. It was, indeed, the soft hour so sweetly described by the poet of the divine drama, reminding the mariner of his latest farewell, and soothing the pilgrim of love with the knell of parting day. But none of this tender influence was felt by the man who stood, panting, on the cliff that overhung the waters. Fury, envy, and malice, contended within him. Why could not he do this? Why, in the many times he had followed her steps, had he never dared to approach her? What spell had been upon him? Had she shrunk at all from the arm which enfolded her? Had she recoiled from the embrace? Might it not have been the same with him? The same blood was in his veins as in Randolph's. Whence came the accursed timidity which held him back? And what did they say? Why could he not hear as well as see? Was there any fascination in Trevethlan's tongue?

And it was he, whom he had learned to hate from his boyhood, his mother's sister's son, whose father cast aside the peasant relatives with contempt; he it was who, in one moment, in a first interview it might be, had achieved a triumph which Michael, with all his opportunities, had never ventured to attempt. But let him look to it. Ruin and shame were impending over his head. It would soon be seen which of them was the better born. The emptiness of his rival's happiness would speedily be discovered. Poverty-stricken and dishonoured, Margaret Basset's son might not be so successful a suitor as the heir of Trevethlan.

Successful! Had he been successful? Had she listened to him with favour? Michael felt that she had. But she would not long exult in her love. She little thought of the chain that was preparing for her. Melcomb, indeed! She need not fear the shallow coxcomb. There was another sort of wooer behind. But for the present her mother must know the liberties taken by the bird. The door of the cage would probably be fastened.

Some such train of ideas flew rapidly through Sinson's perturbed fancy, as he stood a few minutes on the verge of the cliff. He soon turned hastily, and hurried straight across the country to Pendarrel Hall, where he arrived before the young lady who had excited his emotion. He sought its mistress without much ceremony.

"Pray, sir," said she, on seeing him, "what rudeness is this? Did I desire your attendance?"

"No, ma'am," he answered, cringing and trembling. "I beg pardon, ma'am; but I thought you might like to know that Miss Mildred has just met Mr. Trevethlan."

"Well, sir!" Esther said, preserving a composure which bewildered the informant.

"It may be nothing, ma'am, of course," Sinson continued. "But clasping arms, and hands pressed, and lips meeting...."

"Be silent, sir!" exclaimed Mrs. Pendarrel, "and leave the room. I want no tales about Mr. Trevethlan."

In increased astonishment, Michael obeyed. Mildred entered the apartment not very long after.

"My dear Mildred," her mother said, "you should not stay out so late. These February evenings are damp and unhealthy; and besides, dear, you take too long walks. I should be glad if you would confine yourself to the garden. Take a carriage, my love, if you wish for a longer excursion."

Mildred understood her mother well, and knew that this was a command. But amid the rapturous, though confused sensations, with which her heart was thrilling, she did not even notice the coincidence of the injunction with the scene through which she had passed not an hour before. She thought she should be happy at last. She had found a stay to uphold her in the times which she feared were at hand. She had pledged her word, plighted her troth. There was a home ready for her, if her own were made desolate—a haven to receive her, if the storm rose higher than she could bear.

CHAPTER IX.

Quand on est honnête homme, ou ne veut rien devoir
A ce que des parens ont sur nous du pouvoir.
On répugne à se faire immoler ce qu'on aime,
Et l'on veut n'obtenir un cœur que de lui-même.
Ne poussez pas ma mère à vouloir, par son choix,
Exercer sur mes vœux la rigueur de ses droits.
Otez-moi votre amour, et portez à quelqu'autre
Les hommages d'un cœur aussi cher que le votre.

MOLIERE.

So the days passed on; and in due course arrived the one fixed by Mrs. Pendarrel for her great entertainment. March was coming in like a lamb when the appointed morning dawned, the festival having been postponed to nearly the time of the county assizes, for the convenience of Mr. Pendarrel, who was always summoned on the grand jury. Mildred no longer contemplated it with her old alarm, but rather hoped it might afford her an opportunity of coming to an explanation with her suitor of Tolpeden, and so relieve her at once and for ever from his unwelcome addresses. As for Michael Sinson, he had gone to London again.

A very busy day was that at the Hall. Not only the suite of saloons, opening by French windows on a terrace, whence a few steps descended to a lawn diversified by clumps of flowering shrubs, but also, under favour of the genial season, the lawn itself and the neighbouring alleys were prepared for the entertainment of the company. Coloured lamps were dispersed among the bushes, and festoons of the same were hung from branch to branch of the trees which in summer shaded the gravel walks. Arrangements were made also for a display of fireworks. In short, the hostess provided amusement for a very miscellaneous assembly, looking beyond the gaiety of the evening to the maintenance of political influence, and having swept with her invitations half the hundred of West Kerrier.

Her obsequious consort arrived in the course of the day, quitting the cares of office to show civility to his adherents. Unwillingly, indeed, he came, for he hated the country, and would gladly have deferred his visit until the assizes. But his wife required his presence, perhaps, for ulterior views. There was another guest for whom Mildred might hope in vain: no Gertrude was there to gladden her with sisterly affection.

Twilight had scarcely deepened into night when the earliest of the company made their appearance. A worthy civic dignitary from a neighbouring borough, with his wife, and his sons and his daughters, walked in dismay through the splendour of the drawing-rooms to pay his respects to his excellent representative. Alas! that free and independent elector, if, indeed, he survived the shock, has now wept long for his dearly-beloved franchise. As Napoleon has been imagined in shadowy pomp reviewing a spectral army on the plain of Waterloo, may we not fancy that the latest burgesses of Grampound or Old Sarum are summoned from their tombs by the dissolution of a Parliament, meet again in the ruined town-hall, or on the desolate mound, stretch their skeleton hands for the well-remembered compliment, elect a truly British member, partake of an unsubstantial feast, and sink again into their last sleep, in the manner recorded of Bibo, with the honest conviction that, as men and as Englishmen, they have that day done their duty? The mockery would be no greater than of old.

Let not the worthy alderman be disconcerted. Some one must be first at a party, but the intervals between that arrival, and the next, and the next, are always brief, and they become shorter and shorter, until the stream is continuous, and the scattered groups which had been scrutinizing each other are blended together in one great crowd. So it was now: a host of people speedily followed the Pentreaths. There was Sir Simon Rogers, portly and pompous, whose history might be read in the colour of his nose. He was still seeking a successor to the dairy-maid. There was Mr. Hitchins, who had made his fortune by a lucky boring for tin, with his scientific daughter, who, having been down her father's mine, inflicted the descent upon all her partners. To dance with her was almost literally to fall into a pit. There were the Misses Eildon, antiquarian and antiquated. There were sea-board parsons of the old school, who might have called on their congregations to give them a fair start for the wreck. Tres, Rosses, and Pols, Lans, Caers, and Pens, abounded. There was plenty of beauty and plenty of sense. And the throng was illustrated by a few uniforms from the troops on duty in the neighbourhood, still flushed with the glory of the war.

Music lent its inspiration to the throng, and the crowded saloons were all animation. Country dances and quadrilles followed each other in endless succession; and the non-dancing community sauntered to and fro, seeking friends and acquaintance, exchanging compliments and sarcasms, making engagements, indulging in scandal, eternally talking and contributing to the buzz which at a little distance almost overpowered the orchestra. But the prevailing confusion of tongues was slightly stilled when an attendant announced "Mr. Melcomb."

Mildred had remained by her mother's side. She thought there had been something a little peculiar in the observation bestowed upon herself. In the lull which for a moment followed Melcomb's appearance, she supposed she detected its origin. She might read it perhaps more plainly in the faces of two or three worthy dames near her, who, as soon as they heard the name, looked at her with all their might. She passed through the ordeal triumphantly.

Meantime, Melcomb made his way through the press with much show of good-humour and condescension, until he reached the family group. He shook hands warmly with Mrs. Pendarrel, and inflicted a tender pressure on the passive fingers which Mildred extended to receive his salute. Then he fell into what appeared to be a very entertaining conversation with the mother and daughter, and at last led Mildred away to mix in the mazes of the dance.

But although she sustained her part with great spirit, there were not a few quidnuncs, both male and female, who set the young lady down as having anything but her heart in it. Shrewd matrons, thanking their stars that none of their daughters were likely to fall in love with a rake, doubted very much whether Miss Pendarrel was quite pleased with the parental choice. Knowing fathers, congratulating themselves that none of their sons were gamblers, speculated on the grounds of selection.

"They say he's totally ruined," said Mr. Langorel the surgeon, to Mr. Quitch the lawyer.

"Quite, my dear sir. Never heard of anything so complete in all my experience. Know nothing about it professionally, of course. Break off this match, and in a week there would not be a rag left in Tolpeden House, nor a stick in the park."

"What can make them fix on such a fellow?" asked the man of nostrums.

"Well, there's the land to add to the domain," answered the man of deeds. "Extraordinary woman, my dear sir. Covets her neighbour's land like the czar of Russia. The owner goes with it, and diminishes the value, and therefore the cost. And have you not heard what's even now in the wind? Trevethlan Castle——" And mysteriously whispering, the professionals passed on.

"Don't tell me, my dear Mrs. Bonfoy," mumbled the ancient Mrs. Memoirs, "I am old enough—I never disguise the fact, Mrs. Bonfoy—old enough to recollect the mother's marriage. She married in spite, and she spites her children."

"Is he so very bad?" asked Mrs. Bonfoy. "I only believe half what the world says."

"Believe only a hundredth, my dear madam," answered Mrs. Memoirs, "of what it says of him, and you will believe enough to—but no matter."

"Then what can be the reason——?"

"Ah, my dear madam! Tolpeden Park."

"Poor Mrs. Melcomb!"

"Ah!"

Such were the comments, and such the sighs, with which the expected marriage was canvassed in the drawing-rooms of Pendarrel. Its mistress had taken care that the intelligence should be widely diffused, and in all Kerrier there was probably no one who was not cognizant that the match was a settled thing, except the lady whom it chiefly concerned, and the inmates of Trevethlan Castle. Mildred read the news in the faces and the demeanour of the company. Experience enabled her to control her emotion, and she met her destined lord in a manner fully satisfactory both to him and to her mother. The curious of the guests were surprised and disappointed. No scene occurred to gratify their love of scandal. But Mildred's calm deportment concealed a strong resolution. That very night she would have an explanation with Melcomb, and repeat her determination never to be his wife.

She danced with him, and walked with him, and answered his lively badinage with cold civility, continually watching for an opportunity to explain herself. She long watched in vain. As the rooms grew warm, the guests gradually resorted to the lawn and shrubberies, now lighted by the coloured rays of myriad lamps. Thither Melcomb also directed the steps of his partner, who went with pleasure, in the hope that in those less crowded scenes she might obtain the chance which she desired. She even permitted her cavalier to lead her into one of the more sequestered walks, always with the same design. But still she was always foiled. Melcomb maintained such an uninterrupted flow of small-talk, that she could hardly insert a word. It seemed as if he almost divined her intention. Whenever she began a sentence, he stopped her at the first word, assenting beforehand to what he chose to assume she was about to say. And some of the company, observing what seemed the close intimacy of the unhappy couple, were inclined to throw aside their previous suspicions, and to conclude that, after all, the marriage might be one of inclination. Some of the dowagers complimented Mrs. Pendarrel on the cordial affection of her daughter and intended son-in-law, and the wily mother stored up those expressions of sympathy for future use.

At length the discharge of a cannon summoned the admirers of pyrotechny to witness a display of their art. There was a platform and scaffolding erected for the exhibition at the extremity of the lawn. The company thronged around the front, and waited for the show. Nor was it long in commencing. Rockets rushed into the sky, leaving a fiery train behind them, and flinging showers of coloured stars from the highest point of their flight. Bengal lights cast a lurid glare on the trees, and the house, and the faces of the crowd. Wheels of endless variety, and devices of rare skill, excited the admiration, and demanded the applause of the gazers. And the former reached its height, and the latter became loudest, when the final emblem, a true lover's knot surrounded by similar symbols, became visible in lines of fire, beneath a bouquet of rockets and a salvo of cannon.

"Happy will be the day, dear Miss Pendarrel," said Melcomb, forgetting for an instant his prudence, "when that symbol shall become a reality."

"That day," Mildred said, "will never come."

The coxcomb bit his lips, but immediately relapsed into his former persiflage.

From the fireworks, the company went to supper; and after having duly honoured the viands and the wines, returned to the enjoyment of the dance with renewed spirits. Sir Roger de Coverley closed the night's entertainment; and day was already visible in the east before the latest of the party, among whom was Melcomb, arrived at their homes.

The fortitude, which had sustained Mildred during the evening, vanished with the last of the guests. She had designed to come to an explanation with her mother before she slept; but she now felt quite unequal to the task. Lassitude of body increased depression of mind. In sad, almost in solemn accents, she bade her mother and father good night, and retired to rest.

Mrs. Pendarrel, in her secret self, was by no means so well satisfied with her daughter's behaviour, as she pretended to her guests. She had already discovered in Mildred a firmness of character, resembling, if not equalling, her own; and she was rather afraid that this night's tranquillity foreboded a stormy morrow. However, she was not a woman to be easily daunted, and she did not suffer her anxiety to disturb her slumbers.

The day following a party is always dismal. One may remember the second scene in Hogarth's Marriage à la Mode. But the revelry of the night had not disordered the pleasant morning-room, where Mildred presided over the breakfast equipage. It was again a beautiful day. Light clouds were moving gently across the sky; the budding trees were waving in a soft west wind; there was that seeming exuberance of life in the appearance of nature, which is always so exhilarating.

Little influence, however, did it produce on either of the three personages who sat at breakfast. Mr. Pendarrel was engaged in a very prosaic and business-like attack on a dindon aux truffes, a relic of the past night. And he preferred the metropolitan parks to any country lawns and groves. As soon as he had appeased his appetite, or his gourmandism, he went to look to the economy of the establishment. His wife, who enjoyed a true relish for rural pleasures, noted her daughter's quivering eyelids, and trembling fingers, with the consciousness that a scene was coming, in which she might find her part more difficult than she had flattered herself. She had dismissed the breakfast things, and was herself about to leave the room, when Mildred, who was leaning against the side of the window, and gazing wistfully on the garden, turned and arrested her steps.

"Mother," she said, "I must speak with you."

"And what have you to say, Mildred," asked Mrs. Pendarrel, with a freezing smile, "which requires so formal an introduction?"

"I did not know, mother," Mildred replied, "that the party, last night, was to be dedicated, in any way, to my ... my honour. If I had, I would not have been present."

"You will be present, Miss Pendarrel," Esther said, "wherever your father and I choose you to be present."

"Indeed, mother, sorry I am to say it," answered the daughter, mournfully, "I will not, except as a captive. The company shall see my bondage."

"Mildred, let me hear no more of this folly," exclaimed Mrs. Pendarrel. "Captive! Bondage! What romance have you been reading lately?"

"No romance, mother, but myself. Scarcely a month has passed since I told Mr. Melcomb, and you, mother, that I would never be his wife. Do you fancy that month has changed my mind?"

"Twelve hours have not passed, Mildred," said Esther, in the stern tone she could so well adopt, "since here, in the face of half Kerrier, you accepted Mr. Melcomb as your acknowledged suitor. Pshaw, child! Do you think words are the only way of making an engagement? Are you a baby? Why, a hundred people complimented me on the affair last night, and expressed their satisfaction at your evident happiness. And will you dare to tell me, now, that you were acting a lie all that time?"

"Mother, mother!" cried Mildred, "spare such words. You know they are undeserved. So does he. I repeated my determination to him last night."

"What!" Mrs. Pendarrel exclaimed; "but it is no matter. Your faith, your father's, and mine, are alike involved in the fulfilment of this contract, and nothing can prevent it."

"Yes, mother," Mildred said, "I can, and I will."

"You are mistaken in the extent of your abilities, child," Esther said, ironically. "Note me,—I have fixed the day. I have written to your sister. I expect the lawyer here with the writings every day. He has some other business to do for us at the assizes. You will find nerve to sign, I expect. Away with this foolish childishness, Mildred."

"May my hand wither if it takes the pen! Mother, you know my resolution."

With which words Mildred opened the window and passed into the garden.

"So," thought Mrs. Pendarrel, "another check from the house of Trevethlan! I foresaw it all when she trembled on my arm, when she called him her 'cousin.' And they have met! They will rue the day. Beggared and degraded, he might still have maintained his heart, but he has thrown even that to the winds. And what will become of her?—what will become of her?"

A question to which there was very little hope of any favourable answer. The cautious mother had carefully abstained from the least allusion to Mildred's meeting with Randolph, because she knew that by so doing she would probably convert resistance into attack. She recognised in her daughter some of her own spirit, and she trembled to drive her to extremity. Let them await the issue of the coming trial at Bodmin: let them see what became of this intrusive "cousin," before taking any steps which might indicate a suspicion of Mildred's real attachment.

Her daughter strolled sometime listlessly in the garden, in that vacuity of mind which nearly resembles despair. She was like one walking in her sleep. But there were pleasant influences around her. The breeze fell lightly on her cheek, and wafted the dark hair from her forehead. She bent to meet it, like a bird. It came from the sea. Did it remind Mildred of the hawthorns on the cliff? She passed from her saunter on the lawn to her own apartment, and opened her heart in a letter to Mrs. Winston. For some time her pen coquetted with country trifles, as if the writer were trying to escape from an unpleasant topic which nevertheless forced itself into notice, and at last banished every other.

"It has all come true, my dearest sister," she wrote, "all your prediction has come true. Quiet among my flowers and books, *our* books, Gertrude, I was beginning to forget it. All the people paid us their visits and their compliments, and we duly returned them, and of *him* I saw and heard nothing. But you know all about it, for mamma told me she had written to you. It seems he was only to come to our party last night. Everybody we know, with many we can hardly be said to know, was here,—he among the rest; although I had not heard he was in the country, and only learned it from the announcement of his name. I believe I bore it like Gertrude's sister; but oh! dearest, how shall I tell you of my feelings when I saw that every one regarded us as engaged? I hate that *us*. And this morning mamma says my character is compromised. And I am in open and avowed rebellion.

"But this is not all, Gertrude, dear, that I have to tell you. I wish you to guess a little. I have seen our cousin, Mr. Trevethlan, who was at your party, you know. There is the first chapter of my romance. You are coming here soon, and then you shall know more. Till then, and always, believe me, your most affectionate sister,

"Mildred Pendarrel."

CHAPTER X.

Here, a bold, artful, surly, savage race—
Who, only skilled to take the finny tribe,
The yearly dinner, or septennial bribe,
Wait on the shore, and as the waves run high,
On the lost vessel bend their eager eye,
Which to their coast directs its venturous way—
Theirs, or the ocean's, miserable prey.

CRABBE.

"Did you hear what they're saying in the village yonder, Master Randolph?" old Jeffrey asked, as Trevethlan was passing through the gate, on the day after the party. "All the grand doings at Pendar'l?"

Randolph started a little.

"I saw the light in the sky," the warder continued, "and was thinking whose stacks had been fired this time, only it didn't last long now. And they tell me 'twas the squibs and things that were let off to entertain the company like."

"Then there was a party at Pendarrel last night?" Randolph said, in an inquiring tone.

"A party! Indeed I should say there was," Jeffrey answered. "Why, sir, all the country was there from far and wide; all but ours from Trevethlan! And Squire Melcomb of Tolpeden, over the hill yonder, that the folks say is to marry Miss Mildred."

Randolph smiled. "What," said he; "is that so publicly known?"

"It seems like it," Jeffrey said. "But there's strife on foot between our people and Pendar'l. There's a deal of grumbling and threatening down there on the green. They do say as the wedding is fixed for quite soon."

Randolph asked no more, but proceeded on his way. He had not got far from the gates when he met the unrequited lover, Edward Owen. The rustic seemed desirous to say something, for he lingered after making his salute.

"What is it, Edward?" his master asked, "what is the matter?"

"Why, sir, then the folks are just wanting to know what this law-suit is about. You see, sir, we think Pendar'l ha' got quite enough as was ours, and we ought to have some back, rather than give up any more. And the country's a little unquiet just now, and there's no saying exactly what may happen."

"And I am sorry to hear, Edward," Randolph said, "that you have been concerned in the disquiet. It will lead to no good."

"Sir," answered Owen, colouring, "you do not know how I have been urged on. And, for the others, there's a deal wrong in the country at this time."

"But this is not the way to right it, Owen," his master observed. "No good will be done by these night-meetings, and threats, and violence. It is not the way to set things right. You cannot frighten people into doing what you wish. And if you are mixed up with these wrong-doers, you will get into mischief. You will be led further than you meant to go."

Owen muttered some words, either of contrition or of discontent, and pursued his way. It was true that the ferment in the country had considerably increased. The labouring population met almost every night on some point of the moorlands, and although no outrage of much consequence had yet been perpetrated by these mobs, they yet kept up a continual feeling of alarm.

Nor was the danger by any means chimerical. If hitherto no greater mischief had occurred, it was probably rather from the want of sufficient daring in a leader, than of any good will among the mass. And this requisite seemed now likely to be supplied, by an event which happened on the hill-side between Lelant and St. Ives.

A small river there expands into a creek, the shores of which rise rapidly from the water's edge, sometimes cultivated, and sometimes waste, frequently chequered with trees, occasionally broken by masses of rock—always rugged and picturesque. High upon one of the untilled portions, under the shelter of a ledge of slate, stood a low, straggling cottage, constructed of *cob*, and thatched with fern, of which the whitewashed front by day, and a light in the window by night, were visible far out at sea. On the over-hanging rock was a spot showing signs of fire, that commonest and simplest of signals, in by-gone years too often used in these western districts to lure mariners to their destruction; when the skipper, navigating by the fallacious beacon, was startled by the cry of "breakers ahead!" confounded by the crash of his ship's striking, and overpowered by a horde of lawless depredators, unaccustomed in their thirst for plunder, to respect life. But the fierceness of the wreckers, if it still tainted the blood of the peasantry, quailed under the law; and their organ of acquisitiveness now led them to the milder occupation of smuggling. If, in these days, a fire ever burned on the rock in question, it was a friendly warning concerning the fate of some brandy or Hollands, supposed to lurk under the broad lug-sails which the telescope had detected in the offing, and coveted with much zest in many a dwelling on the shore.

This cottage was the abode of Gabriel Denis, a man whose stalwart form and firm step showed that fifty years sat light upon him; while his swarthy, weather-beaten visage, grizzled hair, and resolute eye, told of a life, which hardship and peril had familiarised with endurance and boldness. Some few years before the opening of this narrative, on a dark and stormy night, when a rich landing of spirits and tobacco repaid the country-folks about Zennor for the want of sleep, Denis was found in the morning to have been left behind by the smart schooner which had run boldly under the cliffs in the gloom, and which was then almost beyond the range of glasses. His desertion did not, however, seem to be unexpected by himself, for there were several chests left with him, and also an olive-complexioned woman, whom it appeared he called wife, and a girl about ten years old, whom he styled daughter.

Denis knew very well that there was no danger of a smuggler's being betrayed by the people, yet for some time he lived with great privacy, and thereby attracted the attention which he wished to avoid. In the dusk of evening he used to wander far over the country, and was known not unfrequently to cross the isthmus from St. Ives to Marazion, and stroll along the beach, or over the cliffs, in the direction of Trevethlan Castle. He seemed to listen attentively to the gossip of all the folks about him, and sometimes let fall a remark which indicated a previous acquaintance with the locality. And at such times he would glance round the company as if in search of a recognition.

At length, assured perhaps of his situation, he obtained possession of the cottage we have described, and retired thither with his wife and child. He was evidently deeply attached to the dark-featured woman, and watched all who approached her with extreme jealousy. She was still very handsome, but passionate in temper to excess, and also quick to take affront, partly, perhaps, because she was but imperfectly acquainted with the English language. It required all her husband's watchfulness to avoid perpetual quarrels.

For it was soon discovered that the whitewashed cottage contained a store of those liquors which seem to lead mankind into temptation, universal and irresistible. Now a man, known *sub rosá* to retail smuggled spirits, was not likely to enjoy a perfectly quiet life; a drinking-bout often ends in a battle; Bacchus is the herald of Mars. And whenever such a tumult arose, Gabriel's wife was sure to be vocal in the fray. But Denis possessed a right powerful arm, and knew how to use it: and his customers learned to listen patiently to the strange jargon of Felipa, in wholesome fear of the iron hand of her spouse.

Gabriel's house had become a rendezvous for some of the agitators of the district, who were wont to assemble there at nightfall, and discuss their schemes of outrage under the inspiration of Nantz and Schiedam. Hitherto, these had proved almost wholly abortive; but, as Owen vaguely intimated to the owner of Trevethlan, they now assumed a more threatening aspect, and some inhabitants of that hamlet were foremost among the violent. There had been much question concerning the law-suit between their master and the squire of Pendarrel. Its existence had become generally known, not only by the service of numerous summonses to attend the trial, but also by placards, offering liberal rewards for any information respecting the supposed murder of Mr. Ashton, and the disappearance of Wyley, the missing witness to Margaret Basset's marriage. The rumours regarding that mysterious union, already revived, were stimulated anew by these demonstrations: and the agitation and discontent of the surrounding population were quickened by an indistinct apprehension of some new calamity impending over the family, to which, in spite of everything, they were still strongly attached.

Denis himself had kept aloof from the deliberations, usually held on the turf in front of his dwelling. All he desired was to maintain his wife and child as quietly as he might, on the proceeds of his illicit traffic. But at last, on the very eve of the assizes which were to develope the plot against Trevethlan Castle, the smuggler was doomed to lose his occupation, under circumstances which might have well nigh maddened any man, and much more, one whose life had been like that of Gabriel Denis. Long suspicious, the revenue officers had become at length certain, and swooped upon their prey. The victim blockaded his abode, as best he could, and opposed a gallant resistance to the oppressors. But they were sure of their game, and the defence was fruitless. Yet Denis struggled with them still, when they had effected an entrance: and then, overpowered by numbers, he had the mortification to see the officers, acting evidently on some traitor's information, immediately detect the secret door which led to a natural cave in the rock behind the cottage, and haul forth from that receptacle divers kegs of the precious fluids intended to recreate the lieges of the neighbourhood, but destined for their sovereign's storehouse at Lelant.

Gabriel, in sulky silence, had given up all resistance. But not so his wife. Enraged beyond control, and heedless of her husband's remonstrances, she threw herself furiously upon the captors. It is always difficult to struggle with a woman. Felipa had snatched a pistol from the belt of one of the officers, and in the effort to disarm her, the weapon exploded, and laid her lifeless on the ground. A moment's pause of sorrow and surprise followed, during which Gabriel's little girl threw herself, with loud cries, upon her mother's body, and he himself, after one wild look of despair, flew up the hill-side like the wind.

The officers recovered, and gave chase, but to no effect. The smuggler got clear off. There was nothing to be done but to secure the seizure, and remove the body of the unfortunate victim. The little girl accompanied the train.

The news of the transaction flew far and fast. But it did not prevent the conspirators—if the word is not above their deserts—from resorting to their usual haunt the same evening. They lay, six or seven in number, in various attitudes on the turf in front of the ruined cottage, in the irresolute and objectless mood of which many a plot has perished. Agreeing in a desire, either for wanton mischief or for their neighbours' goods, they could not make up their minds how to begin. The cowardice, which always attends the doing of wrong, lay heavy on their hearts, and made their hands powerless.

But Gabriel Denis came down the hill and joined the criminal divan. Trained in a lawless life, burning with the desire for revenge, heedless of the manner, he brought into the assembly the passion and energy for which it had before sought in vain. He listened awhile to the incoherent gabble of the agitators, and then startled their indecision by a direct proposition of his own. His speech was cold, and his words were few; yet there was not a man who heard him, but knew that he meant what he said. And when the little party dispersed, it was with a confident feeling, that the next meeting of their adherents at Castle Dinas would not terminate in the same inoffensive manner as previous musters of the same nature.

CHAPTER XI.

Peace, brother, be not over-exquisite
To cast the fashion of uncertain evils;
For grant they be so, while they rest unknown,
What need a man forestall his date of grief,
And run to meet what he would most avoid?

MILTON.

The summonses referred to in the last chapter had been very widely distributed among all those of the tenantry of Trevethian, who had been cotemporaries of poor Margaret Basset. They were, in fact, issued almost at random, in order that the defendant in the trial might have at hand every possible means of rebutting his adversary's case. But they were not confined to the dependents of the castle: old Maud Basset and her daughter, Cecily, also received subpœnas, and Michael Sinson was greatly startled by being served with one himself.

Mr. Winter had offered some early opposition to Randolph's desire to hurry on the matter without delay. His experience taught him to look with hope to the discovery of a clue to the plaintiff's intentions, and he would gladly have avoided the risk even of a temporary defeat. There was, too, ample reason for postponement, in the chance, however slight it might be, of finding the missing witness, Wyley; and in the short space, there would otherwise intervene, for ascertaining as much as possible of the clergyman, Mr. Ashton. All these considerations, however, gave way to the urgency with which Randolph insisted on despatch. And as there is a way, even in law, where there is a will, and the other side were at least as anxious for an issue, the cause was brought to a condition, for trying at the assizes which were now commencing.

It may not be uninteresting to the reader, to see the exact position, stripped of technicalities, in which the parties stood at going into court. The question between them was one of inheritance merely, and of a very simple kind. Randolph's great grandfather left two sons by different marriages, Arthur, the eldest, and Philip, the present claimant of the property at stake. Arthur was the father of only one son, Henry. It will be seen, therefore, that in default of any will, and of Henry's dying without family, the estates would revert to Philip. There was no will to interfere, for Henry, in his, merely appointed guardians of his children, and made no bequests. He considered it a matter of course that the children would inherit. And so they would, if the marriage of which they were the offspring, were legal. But if this marriage were not duly performed, or the children supposititious, Philip would become heir to the property.

It was, therefore, almost self-evident, that the claimant's case would rest upon the insufficiency of Randolph's father's marriage. So to this point was directed the main attention of his legal advisers. But every presumption was in favour of its perfect legality. All the dark suggestions which subtilty could imagine, vanished one after another, in the light thrown upon them by Henry Trevethlan's own conduct. If there were a fraud, it must have been without his cognizance, for it would have defeated his supposed object. But if he were not privy, what motive could be ascribed to any other party? It was impossible, for obvious reasons, to impute anything of the kind to the friends of the bride. Baffled in every conjecture, Mr. Winter could only take means for procuring the presence of everybody, who, by any remote contingency, might be able to contribute to the overthrow of the claimant's case.

For in this sort of action the parties meet at the trial totally ignorant of each other's intentions. For instance, in this case the claim might be made, either under an alleged will, or a sale and conveyance of the property, or on the ground that the holder was not the legitimate heir. And supposing the first case, the defendant might say, either that the will was forged, or was made when the testator was of unsound mind, or was revoked by a later. So wide is the field for surprise. And consequently it frequently happens, that the title to a disputed estate is very far from established by a single verdict; but that in a series of trials, the parties alternately upset one another's successive positions, until the ground is exhausted, and the matter finally set at rest.

We have seen that the approach of the contest caused great excitement in the hamlet of Trevethlan. It was an agitation not unmixed with shadowy dread. The presentiments and forebodings which had long afforded a theme for the village guidance, were discussed more anxiously than ever. The old people recollected every little coincidence attending a death in the family, or the severance of an estate, and detected something parallel at the present time. Some aged folks listened at night for the wailing cries which ought to echo around the old grey towers on the eve of a calamity; and when none such mingled with the gentle sighing of the west wind, they interpreted this very softness into a sign, declared the unnatural warmth of the season was a certain token of ill, and remembered some similar year when disaster visited the castle. Of course, this state of feeling reacted within its walls, and revived the terrors of the domestics. In spite of Helen's contradiction to Mercy Page, the wiseacres of the hamlet insisted on peopling the gloomy galleries with visitors from another world, and some of the more eager occasionally watched the windows at night, in the hope of being terrified and having a story to tell.

It had been well if these night-fancies were all that disturbed the people. But not a few of them were speculating already on what should be done, in case the forebodings were verified by the result. And here, had it been known, was a veritable cause for alarm. Randolph himself would, perhaps, have trembled, if he had been aware what his dependents were meditating, as they supposed for his advantage, but at all events for their own satisfaction.

For some time after his interview with Mildred, the gloom and moroseness which beset him previously, had vanished. Strong in the hope and trust inspired by that meeting, he became frank and unreserved in his intercourse with the villagers, lively and agreeable in his circle at home. Helen and Polydore rejoiced at the change, without knowing its origin. It showed itself in the smile with which he heard Jeffrey's announcement of Miss Pendarrel's approaching marriage. "Simple people!" he might think, "how little you know on the subject!" But as the day of trial came quite near, some of his former agitation naturally returned: he shunned the conversation of the peasants, and became once more abstracted and silent at home. Again did the rustics note the gloom upon his brow, and whisper among their other prognostications that their master's doom was written in his face; but he should not fall unavenged.

Nor was Michael Sinson more at his ease. He had gone to London before the party at Pendarrel, to consult Mr. Truby, and to see his bondman, Everope. It was essential that he should maintain his influence over the latter unbroken, and keep him well prepared for the part he was to play. He was greatly startled himself by being summoned as a witness for the defendant. He had intended, indeed, to go down to the assizes, but he did not mean to appear. He should remain in the background, while his creature did his work. He trembled to think of the confessions into which he might be driven or led by the searching questions of counsel; but still more he alarmed himself by imagining that his opponents had obtained some clue to his design, and that some strange exposure awaited him in court. He was, however, now so deeply involved, that he could only strengthen himself with his old hopes, and abide the issue in patience.

His aged grandmother was at least as much perplexed as himself. Ever since her favourite Michael had dropped his dark hint in her ear respecting the marriage, she had harped upon the subject in her muttered soliloquies, and ruminated upon it as she swung to and fro in her rocking-chair. And in the confusion of her ideas she fancied, on receiving her summons, that there was a plot on foot by which the Trevethlans desired to free themselves from the connection with her family, and willingly transferred to Randolph the passing reproaches with which at times she upbraided Michael Sinson. It was idle to reason with her.

"Ay, Squire Trevethlan," she cried to him one day, as he was strolling in the neighbourhood of her lodge, in the vain hope of quieting his renewed anxiety by another meeting with Mildred. "The son steps worthily in the path of the father! And so thou wouldst be quit of the peasant blood, wouldst thou? Wouldst disown thy kindred? But na, na,—the ties are too strong. It's none so easy to break a mother's memory. My Margaret was fit for the wife of a king, and more than fit to be the mother of such as thee."

"Who has been talking to you now, dame?" Randolph asked. "Who has been putting these notions in your head? Did I ever wish to disown her? Would I not give anything to bring her back? Would I not love her and honour her? And did I not tell you I had seen her, and she smiled upon me? She has come often since, and always with the same sweet smile."

He fancied the old woman had been tampered with, and wished to know the particulars.

"I dinna believe thee," Maud answered; "I dinna believe it at all: and they say she has walked in the castle indeed, but no with a smiling face. She came to warn thee, grandson Randolph. And well she might. Well she might wander there, where she was let to pine and pine, and no one of all her own people let to come nigh her. And most of all now, when her own son would put her out of her rightful place. Shame upon him!"

"'Tis because I am her son," Randolph expostulated, "that you should not believe these tales, Dame Basset. What! do you not know that if she were not my father's wife, the castle and everything we have pass away from my sister and me? And have we not asked you to come to the trial to speak for us, and prove the marriage? Who is it has put these stories in your head?"

"I cannot understand it at all," the old woman answered. "Why should I speak yon for thy side? Why shouldst thou come to me? Have not thy people put me and mine out from among them? I cannot understand it at all."

"But at least, dame," Randolph urged, "you will say it was a good marriage?"

"Every one knows that," she said. "Let me see the one that denies it. But go, go. Said I not there was a dark hour at hand for thy house? It is near, near. I said it was written in thy face. It is clearer and plainer now. Thou beguiled me with that tale of her smile, but I heard the rights o't since. There'll never be peace 'twixt thine and mine."

And so saying, she retreated into the lodge, and left Randolph, puzzled, but not annoyed by her unfounded suspicions. Her words were so far satisfactory, that they showed how strong was her confidence in the validity of the marriage.

At the opening of the assizes, Polydore Riches and the steward went to Bodmin to be in constant communication with Winter and his counsel. The worthy lawyer had himself already made a flying visit to Trevethlan, for the purpose of investigating the evidence a little more closely. He was rather dismayed on finding at every turn that the rumours current at the time of the marriage were still so fresh in the memory of the people. "Faith!" said he to himself, "we have wasted our subpœnas pretty freely! Why, there's scarcely a person out of the castle I shall dare to call!" Moreover, he had been disheartened somewhat by the intelligence he had gained respecting Mr. Ashton, as it seemed to show that there were but few qualities in his character to prevent him from being a party to a trick, provided it were profitable to himself. The placards offering a reward for news of Wyley had called forth no information.

Randolph persisted, against the advice of the chaplain, in attending the trial himself. He was resolved to hear the case against him from the lips of the witnesses. Polydore was grieved, thinking that if the issue was favourable the trifling delay in communicating it would be unimportant, and if it were adverse, its effect might be softened. Besides which, there might be incidents in the proceedings of a painful nature, from which the defendant had better be away. But a wilful man must have his way, and Randolph would not be overruled.

The evening before his departure he sat with Helen, feverish and excited, in their favourite turret-room, overlooking the sea. The delightful weather still continued, and they kept the window open long after dark.

"Do you remember, Helen," the brother asked, "how we were sitting here, side by side, as we are now, when there came that letter, insulting us with the offer of alms?"

"Dear Randolph," Helen answered, "you know I would have thought differently of that letter. But why should I remember it now?"

"Because, my sister, to-morrow's trial may place us in need of alms," he replied. "I do not know why it is, but from the very first I have thought we should be beaten in this suit. I have been haunted ever by the idea that the pittance which I then disdained might become necessary to us. It seems to me a natural consequence of the refusal. Are they so proud? it was said—they shall be humbled."

"But we shall not, Randolph," his sister said. She was saddened by the bitterness with which he spoke. "We shall not be humbled. Not in the sense you mean. We shall not have to seek assistance. The schemes which we plotted for the restoration of our house, may they not be revived to minister to our necessities? See, when that letter came, you asked, why have we desponded. And shall we despond now? Believe me, my brother, I am prepared for the worst."

"If that were all," Randolph said, "if poverty and the loss of our dear home were all, bitter as it would be, it might be borne. But our father or our mother, the one or the other, will be defamed, and our name dishonoured. Helen, if this suit goes against us, and I survive the day, it will only be to brand our opponents with the villany by which they win, not with any notion of supporting a life I shall abhor."

He disengaged himself from her arm as he finished speaking, and leant against a division of the open window. But she followed him, and laid her hand upon his shoulder.

"And me, Randolph," she said; "you are a man; but what will become of me?"

"Of you, dearest!" he exclaimed. "Did you ever think, my sister, of her I mentioned but now? She died before you had left your cradle. Scarcely as a baby even could you know her. But I was nearly three years old. And the memory has dwelt secretly in my breast, and it has come back to me of late. I have seen her face in my dreams, sometimes smiling and sometimes sorrowful, but always full of love. I have thought she came to implore me to protect what was her only dowry, her good name, or to console me and make me hopeful under a passing misfortune. And then, when I remember the attack which is to be made to-morrow, my heart burns, and I say what I do not mean. But you, dearest! I shall live to be with you, whatever may befall."

And so saying, he bent down and kissed his sister.

"Do you see that bright planet?" he continued. "I have called it my star. It has shone on some of the happiest moments of my life. A childish fancy, sister, but it pleases me. The sight of it, clear and unclouded as it is now, breathes promise of joy to my heart. Trust me, sister, whatever may happen in this cause, there is comfort in store for us yet."

CHAPTER XII.

King John. Our strong possession, and our right, for us.

Elinor. Your strong possession, much more than your right;
Or else it must go wrong with you, and me:
So much my conscience whispers in your ear,
Which none but Heaven, and you, and I, shall hear.

SHAKSPEARE.

Early the following day, Randolph sprang into the carriage which was to convey him to Bodmin, where his fate would, for the present at least, be decided. He bade his sister good-bye in a cheerful voice, but with a gloomy countenance, and she staid at the hall-door until the gates had closed upon his way. The carriage rattled down the descent of the base-court, and round the village green; and the few rustics, who met it with respectful salutes, shook their heads doubtfully as they looked after it, and foreboded no joyful return.

But the sun was shining bright and warm; the hedges were bursting prematurely into leaf; the birds were singing merrily; all the influences of nature concurred to raise the spirits of the wayfarer, and inspire him with hope. He became interested in the journey, and his presentiments of evil vanished away.

In the evening Randolph entered the precincts of the county town, and was driven to the hotel, where he had appointed to meet Polydore Riches; and glad he was to escape from the bustle and noise of the busy town to the parlour engaged by the chaplain. He was also glad to find that Polydore, anticipating his wishes, had provided against any visits. He did not even desire to see Rereworth.

The next morning, after a slight and hasty breakfast, he took the chaplain's arm, and proceeded through the lively and crowded streets to the court-house. No one knew him, and he passed along entirely unheeded. But the cause had excited very considerable interest. The story of the quarrel between Mrs. Pendarrel and her early suitor was by no means forgotten, and the rumour of her new attack upon Trevethlan Castle had attracted no little attention. The circumstances of its late owner's marriage were recalled to mind, and regarded with various kinds of criticism. The lovers of scandal flocked to the court-house in hope of gratifying their spleen, and the vague reports that were circulated respecting the grounds of the plaintiff's claim promised amusement to the admirers of piquant private history. People in general remembered how large a portion of the hereditary estates of Trevethlan had passed under the sway of the rival house, and looked perhaps with trembling pity on the last relic of the old domain; and even the peasantry might feel an interest in the fulfilment of the popular prophecy. So all these feelings combined to swell the assemblage which crowded the court. Polydore introduced his old pupil to a seat on the bench; from thence Randolph exchanged a grave bow with Seymour Rereworth, and took his place with a countenance whose constrained tranquillity was very much at variance with the emotion which it concealed.

Shortly afterwards the judge made his appearance, and the rumour which had pervaded the crowd gradually subsided. There were some questions asked, and points decided, respecting a cause which had been tried the preceding day; and, as soon as this conversation was finished, the clerk of assize, in a low methodical tone, read from his cause-list, Doe d Pendarrel *v.* Trevethlan; counsel on each side nodded; a jury was sworn well and truly to try the issue between the parties; the plaintiff's junior briefly described the nature of the action, and amidst perfect silence, his leader rose to state the case he should lay before the court.

He began by lamenting the painful duty which devolved upon him on the present occasion, and begging the jury to forget whatever they might have heard of previous disputes between the families whose names appeared in this record. It was too frequently the case, in suits of this nature, that the parties were nearly connected. Passing from this introduction, he observed that in such actions they had also frequently to inquire into a long and tedious pedigree, or to make a fatiguing investigation of documentary evidence. No task of the kind awaited them here. The case he had to present was exceedingly short and simple, and rested mainly on the testimony of a single witness. And however extraordinary the story which this witness would tell, he was sorry to say that it was strongly confirmed by the conduct and circumstances of him whom it impeached. The action was brought to obtain possession of Trevethlan Castle and the surrounding domain. The jury were probably aware that the real claimant in the cause, Mr. Philip Trevethlan Pendarrel, had assumed the last name in addition to his own, on his marriage with an heiress of large fortune in the county. He now preferred his claim as the younger son of Hugh Trevethlan, Esquire, of Trevethlan Castle, from whom the defendant also deduced his title; so that it would be unnecessary to go any further back. Having established the claimant's birth, it would, however, become requisite to show that there were now no lawful descendants of his elder brother, or rather half brother, Arthur Trevethlan, the alleged grandfather of the defendant. Now it was admitted that from this Arthur, the estates in question descended legally to his son Henry; but with the latter, it was maintained the succession in that line terminated. They would observe that Henry, the late possessor, only died towards the close of the previous year, which would account for no steps having been taken sooner. Now it was well known that, for many years before his death, all intercourse between him and his uncle, the claimant, had entirely ceased; and that in fact they were not on those terms of friendship which should exist between such near relations. It was also known that for a long time the late Mr. Trevethlan lived a very retired life at his castle, and never went into society at all. Further, he had fully attained the age of forty before there was any rumour or pretence that he had contracted a marriage. But about this time, it is suggested that if he died without offspring, the estates would either revert to the relative from whom he was alienated, or he must bequeath them to a stranger; and the jury would readily perceive the feelings which would be excited by either alternative. Accordingly, in order to avoid them both, it would seem that Mr. Trevethlan then contemplated matrimony, and that a certain ceremony was performed between him and one Margaret Basset, the daughter of a small farmer upon his estate. The defendant in this action is the son of this Margaret Basset. "Now, gentlemen," continued the counsel, "I need not unpleasantly press upon your attention the circumstances under which the late Mr. Trevethlan might have found it convenient to repudiate this pretended marriage. They did not arise, and the marriage was not repudiated. Neither, so far as we can learn, was it ever confirmed in a legal manner:—it was never properly registered. The only mention of it in the parish records occurs in the account of the christening of the defendant, who is described (I read from an attested copy) as the 'son of Henry and Margaret Trevethlan, who were married by special licence, in this parish, by the Reverend Theodore Ashton, on the 3rd of September, in the previous year, in the presence of —— Wyley, and of Maud Basset.' This entry is signed Henry Trevethlan, Margaret Trevethlan, Maud Basset. The questions naturally arise,—where is the signature of the officiating clergyman?—where is that of the witness Wyley? And the answer to these inquiries is found in the real history of the circumstances attending this alleged marriage. The ceremony was performed in private, within the castle, but without the presence even of any of the household; within twenty-fours afterwards, the clergyman alleged to have performed it disappeared, and was supposed to be murdered. The only male witness also vanished; and the only other witness was the mother of the pretended bride, who is still living, and will probably be called before you by my learned friend."

Here the speaker was interrupted by a scuffle in the court, and the shrill voice of Maud Basset. "He lies!" she screamed. "My Margaret *was* married. Let me see the one who says the contrary." But the old woman was speedily removed.

"Gentlemen," the counsel resumed, "both you and I can understand and sympathize with the feeling which prompted that interruption. I was describing the mysterious privacy with which this pretended marriage was—I will not say solemnized—but performed. It is perhaps generally supposed that the poor old woman who interrupted me is the sole survivor of those who were present at the scene; but it is not so. We shall to-day produce another. We shall call before you the person who acted the part of the clergyman:—not Mr. Ashton, gentlemen, nor a clergyman at all."

There was a great sensation in the court at these words. And if any one among the audience had then looked at Randolph, he could not fail to have been struck by the ghastly rigidity of his features. But all were too deeply interested by the announcement which they had heard to attend to anything else.

The plaintiff's counsel proceeded to say that he need not anticipate the details this witness would relate;—they would completely overthrow any claim founded upon this alleged marriage. It would be for his learned friends to show any subsequent ground for their title, if such they had. But unless they did so, he should confidently look for a verdict at the hands of the jury; and, as he should undoubtedly have another opportunity of addressing them, he would not now trouble them at greater length.

A considerable rumour pervaded the court at the close of this speech, but soon yielded to the low calls for order. There followed some technical evidence respecting Mr. Pendarrel's descent, and the deaths of his brother and nephew, of no particular interest, and then the leader who had addressed the jury, re-awakened attention by desiring the crier to call Lewis Everope. Rereworth looked at the spendthrift, as he quietly took the oath, with utter astonishment, not knowing what to think. The examination began.

"What are you, Mr. Everope?"

"I belong to no profession, but have been nominally a student of the law."

"You were educated at —— University, I believe, sir?"

The witness uttered an intimation of assent.

"Were you acquainted, while there, with a gentleman named Ashton,—Theodore Ashton?"

"I was."

"How long is this ago? To a year or two?"

"Twenty-three or four years. I do not exactly recollect."

"Mr. Ashton was your senior, I believe?"

"Considerably. In fact our acquaintance was very slight."

"What became of him afterwards, do you know?"

"He took orders, and quitted the University."

"Did you ever see him after you had left college?"

"I did."

"Be so good as to tell the jury under what circumstances."

"I was making a pedestrian tour through the western part of this county, and met him unexpectedly in the neighbourhood of Marazion."

"What year was this? And month? Do you remember?"

The witness mentioned those of Henry Trevethlan's marriage.

"Did you visit Mr. Ashton at his then residence?"

"Yes."

"Well, I believe that was no great distance from Trevethlan Castle. Tell the jury anything that passed between you and your friend, having reference to that building or its inhabitants."

"I naturally asked Mr. Ashton some question respecting it, and he told me there was a strange story on foot about its owner, who wished to play the trick attempted by Thornhill, in the Vicar of Wakefield. He had applied to Ashton on the subject, but the latter told him, that if he performed the ceremony, the result would be the same as in the tale. But Ashton was to have a considerable fee, and he asked me to personate him, representing that the affair was only a joke, and that, if there were any family, Mr. Trevethlan would certainly confirm it legally. And I being young, and not at the time aware of the consequences, ultimately consented to what he proposed."

"Well, sir, and what followed?"

"Ashton said he could arrange for the affair to take place the next day———"

"What day was that?"

"It was the third of September. Ashton instructed me how to present myself at the castle in his name. No one who would be present, he said, knew him, except Mr. Trevethlan, who expected something of the kind, and I looked considerably older than I was. And an intended witness to the wedding would conduct me."

"And what happened afterwards?"

"I went to the castle with the witness in question, and Mr. Trevethlan introduced himself to me without any remark, and presented a young woman as his intended bride. There was also another woman present, who, he said, was her mother. Mr. Trevethlan produced a document, which he stated to be a licence for a special marriage, but I did not look at it; and read the marriage service as fast as I could from a prayer-book which was given me. When it was over, Mr. Trevethlan handed me a sum of money, which I delivered to Ashton, and quitted the neighbourhood without delay, for I did not like my part in the business."

"I should think not," said the counsel. "Pray, sir, do you recollect any particular incident at this ceremony?"

"Only, that in my confusion I dropped the ring, and the bride's mother muttered something which I did not hear."

"You have not mentioned the name of the bride?"

"Margaret Basset."

"You were not in holy orders at that time?"

"Neither then nor since."

The plaintiff's counsel here sat down, and Rereworth's leader rose. The cross-examination was very long and severe.

"So, sir," it began, "do you know that you have just confessed yourself guilty of felony?"

"I know it now," Everope said, "but I did not know it at the time."

"And you might have been transported for fourteen years?"

"So I am told."

Counsel then ran him hard and fast through all the details of the scene he had described. Asked for descriptions of the castle, of the room, of the persons. Turned back upon his own family. Where were they at the time? How did he correspond with them? Where were they now? He was on bad terms with them. How was that? He said he was of no profession. Was he a man of private fortune? How did he live? Who paid his expenses in coming here? What did he expect beyond? Then suddenly round again. Where did he sleep the night before the mock-marriage? At Marazion? What was the name of the inn? Where did he go afterwards? From what place did he come? Then abruptly, did he know Michael Sinson? How long had he been acquainted with him? What intercourse had been between them? Had Michael promised him anything for coming here? Again back to his career at the university; his subsequent life; his present circumstances. And once more to Trevethlan Castle; again to describe the almost incredible proceeding to which he had so distinctly sworn, and all the circumstances of his intimacy with Ashton.

But this cross-questioning failed in materially shaking Everope's evidence in chief. He was forced into a considerable exposure of himself; but, perhaps, even after making the allowance which he claimed for youth and inexperience, the mere avowal of his participation in so detestable a plot was sufficiently damning, without any aggravation. It was evidently not improbable that, at so distant a time, he might not well remember the details of the scene. Only once did he seem likely to be overturned.

"Have you ever been in the neighbourhood since?" he was asked.

"Once."

"And when was that?"

"About six weeks ago."

"Were you alone?"

"No, I was with Michael Sinson, whom you have mentioned."

"Indeed! And why did you come? You need not hesitate."

"I came to refresh my memory," Everope answered boldly.

"And to good purpose," counsel said, "for it has been very convenient."

But the leader was on the point of sitting down, when Rereworth gave him a slip of paper, and he asked one more question.

"Pray, sir, are you personally acquainted with the defendant in this action?"

"No," Everope said.

"It is I!" Randolph exclaimed, rising from his seat, and fixing the spendthrift.

"Order, order," was murmured, and the interrupter, who drew the attention of every one in court, sat down. It was a few moments before the excitement occasioned by this incident had subsided. There was a general stir to obtain a second look of the unknown possessor of Trevethlan Castle.

"Morton!" the witness had meantime exclaimed, showing signs of confusion for the first time.

"You do know him, then?" said the counsel, and sat down.

But the question did not seem to be advantageous to the defendant's interest.

"What do you know of Mr. Trevethlan?" Everope's former examiner asked, having heard his exclamation.

"I knew that gentleman slightly in the Temple by the name of Morton, as a student for the bar."

The re-examination was short. Some additional formal evidence was given; and the only other material witness on this side was the coroner, who proved the circumstances of the supposed murder of Mr. Ashton, and the disappearance of Wyley. With this evidence, the case for the plaintiff, of which we have only reported the portion on which the jury would have eventually to form their judgment, was closed; and the court adjourned for a short period.

CHAPTER XIII.

Ah, Richard, with the eyes of heavy mind,
I see thy glory, like a shooting star,
Fall to the base earth from the firmament.
Thy sun sets weeping in the lowly west,
Witnessing storms to come, war, and unrest;
Thy friends are fled to wait upon thy foes,
And crossly to thy good all fortune goes.

SHAKSPEARE.

Randolph Trevethlan never stirred from his seat during the suspension of the proceedings. When they were resumed, his counsel argued at some length, that even if the tale which they had heard were true, the marriage so contracted would be valid, and that therefore the plaintiff had failed in making out his case. The other side were stopped in their reply by the judge, who said, that while the court would listen with patience to any argument intended to save an innocent woman from the effect of a fraudulent marriage, that could not be considered the point in question here; the imputed object being to interfere with the rights of the heir presumptive by securing a family; and that, therefore, without expressing any opinion upon what might be considered an undecided point, he should not stop the case. So Rereworth's leader proceeded to address the jury for the defence.

He began by a skilful and minute analysis of Everope's narrative, in which he exhibited its incredibility in a strong light, and heightened it by a continual reference to the worthlessness of the witness's character as exposed by himself. He pointed out his connection with Michael Sinson, a person in the employment of the claimant's family, and a nephew of the late Mrs. Trevethlan. From him, therefore, Everope could have obtained all the particulars which he pretended to know of his own experience. He would be called before the court, and the jury would judge whether the tale had not been concocted between the two. Sinson had motives of his own for hostility to the family of Trevethlan, which would be heard from his own lips. He did not impute to the claimant any cognizance of the fraud, by which he maintained the claim had been attempted to be established. Departing from this point, he said he should show, by indisputable evidence, that the late Mr. Trevethlan never contemplated the baseness which had been attributed to him, could not possibly have suspected any flaw in his marriage, and always treated Margaret as his lawful wife, and his children as lawfully born; for, first, he strongly desired that his own chaplain would perform the ceremony, as they would hear from that gentleman himself; secondly, if, as suggested by the plaintiff, his object had been to make sure of barring the present claim, he would have caused the marriage to be repeated before the birth of his first child; and thirdly, if he had had any suspicion that his children would not inherit by descent, he would have assuredly provided for them by will. But although his estates belonged to him in fee, he had bequeathed them nothing, dying, as it might be said, intestate; he had always treated Margaret as his wife, and had never expressed the slightest doubt of the perfect formality of his marriage. By his own conduct he had thus defeated the very design which was imputed to him, and his own alleged proceedings would have brought about that result which he was said to have sought to avoid, the succession, namely, of the present claimant. In the face of so much incoherency, was it possible, for one moment, to entertain so incredible a tale as that which had been heard from a witness of so very disreputable a character? If such testimony could prevail, no household would be safe.

Now, he should produce the licence under which the marriage took place; he should—despite the incident which Everope had stated as occurring, and which he had probably learned from Michael Sinson—call before them Maud Basset, the mother of Margaret, the only known surviving witness of the ceremony, and she would tell them—they had heard her exclamation in court—that it was a good marriage; he should also call several members of the household of Trevethlan Castle, who would swear they always regarded it as such; and he should show that the children had been christened as the lawful offspring of Henry and Margaret Trevethlan; and again he repeated, that if the unsupported and monstrous testimony of a single individual of bad reputation were permitted to countervail so strong a chain of presumption no union could be secure, and any of his hearers would be liable to have his children disinherited and their names stigmatized by any villain who would forswear himself for hire.

Let the jury consider the story they had heard. That a gentleman of high character and station, under circumstances entirely different from those in Goldsmith's famous story, wishing to form a marriage which he might either affirm or repudiate subsequently, should dare to apply to a stranger, a clergyman of the church, to assist him in so nefarious a design,—that this clergyman, far from expressing any indignation, should merely suggest a little difficulty,—that, by a coincidence sufficiently remarkable, this Everope, discarded by his family, living by his wits, should at that very time encounter his old college acquaintance,—that to him Ashton should immediately relate the business, and invite his co-operation,—that this precocious villain should at once accept the mission,—that Mr. Trevethlan should receive him without question or surprise,—that he should perform the impious mockery he had described,—that, needy and profligate, he should keep so valuable a secret for so long a time,—that at length, by another singular coincidence, he should fall in with a dependent of the family to whom it was so important; should tell the story apparently as an excellent joke; should for the first time become aware of its worth, and should sell himself to give the evidence they had heard to-day—Yes: indignation had diverted him from the picture he was drawing to the real motive under which the witness acted.

But let the jurors turn from this view of the subject to the one he should now present to them. Let them see Mr. Trevethlan, when, for reasons entirely beside the question at issue, he had decided on marrying a person of inferior station, applying to his chaplain, as a matter of course, to perform the ceremony. Let them see him, on that gentleman's declining, preferring the same desire to this Mr. Ashton, then resident in the neighbourhood. Let them suppose the ceremony to have been really and duly performed by him, as it appears recorded in the register of baptisms. Let them recollect the disappearance of Ashton, and of Wyley, the witness. Let them see how two children were borne by Mrs. Trevethlan, and duly christened by the chaplain of the castle. Let them then turn to the conduct of her relations. Let them imagine the hopes raised, the desires excited by their great connection. Let them note one of these relatives permitted to hang about the castle as a sort of companion to the young heir. Let them suppose certain presumption to grow up, and to be suddenly checked by the expulsion of all the race. Let them conceive the consequent exasperation, and heighten it by an unfounded suspicion that the exalted peasant-woman was ill-used. Let them consider such feelings as still rankling when Michael Sinson enters the service of the claimant in this action. Let them think of him as actuated both by hope of reward and desire of revenge, devising this subtile scheme, and seeking only an agent to accomplish it. Let them find him meeting the ruined scoundrel, whom they had heard that day, and he thought they would have little difficulty in unravelling the dark plot, which was now, for the first time, publicly developed against the well-being, the happiness, and the good fame of an old and distinguished and honourable family.

At the close of this address, Michael Sinson was called into the witness-box, and examined by Rereworth.

"You are a relation, I believe, of the late Mrs. Trevethlan?"

"A nephew of the late Margaret Basset."

The witness was then led on, by further questions, to describe the hopes excited in his family by the marriage now in dispute; the manner in which he was allowed to hang about Trevethlan Castle; the offence which his demeanour gave to its owner, and the expulsion of his relations from their farm. Fencing with his examiner, he at first affected to treat this circumstance with indifference, but was forced by degrees into a confession of his bitter and rankling mortification.

"And so, sir," Rereworth suddenly asked, "all your family considered this marriage to be perfectly good?"

"It was for their interest," Sinson said, stammering.

"For their interest, sir!" Seymour exclaimed indignantly. "Why, sir, was not Mrs. Trevethlan's good name at stake?"

"My poor relative has been dead for a long time," the witness answered.

"And it is her nephew who comes forward to shame her in her grave! You are now in the service of Mr. Pendarrel, the real claimant in this action?"

"Of Mrs. Pendarrel."

The answer produced a slight titter in the court.

"What does Mrs. Pendarrel pay you for getting up her case?"

Sinson hesitated for some time, and made no answer.

"Do you hear, sir?" Rereworth continued. "What is to be your hire for slandering your mother's sister?"

The plaintiff's counsel interposed, and protested against his learned friend's so discrediting his own witness.

"I consider," the witness said, having recovered himself, "that my unfortunate relative was deceived in the business. It was no fault of hers."

Rereworth now turned to Michael's connection with Everope. Asked how the acquaintance began; how long it had lasted; how the spendthrift came to communicate the story which he told in court; what Sinson knew of his habits and associates; whether he provided him with a maintenance? Then he reverted to the journey into Cornwall, of which Everope had given so frank an explanation; and concluded by again questioning the witness respecting any expectation of reward which he entertained or had held forth as the consequence of success in this action.

"Do you expect any reward at all, sir?" Michael was asked, in cross-examination. "Have any promises been made to you?"

"No," he answered, "I have been only doing my duty, and expect nothing."

"And have you, in fact, held out any expectations to the witness Everope?"

"None whatever."

"Well, sir, is it not matter of notoriety that there was great doubt about this pretended marriage?"

"Certainly. It has been thrown in my teeth a hundred times."

Little profit had this witness brought to the defendant. Maud Basset, who had been detained out of court since her interruption of the proceedings, was now summoned into the box.

"You are the mother of the late Mrs. Trevethlan, madam?"

"Sure and I am. Of my own Margaret. But I dinna understand it at all."

"You recollect your daughter's marriage, Mrs. Basset?"

"And a proud day was that for me," the old woman replied, "when the squire asked for her to be his wife. But my Margaret was fit to be a queen. Woe's me that he beguiled me, that she should be married only to be murdered."

"You were present at the marriage, I believe, madam?"

"Of course I was. Where else should her mother be? And he all so cold and stately like, and she weeping and crying so. I might have known what would come of it. I saw it all with my own eyes."

"Do you remember the name of the clergyman, Mrs. Basset?"

"Ashton it was—Theodore Ashton. The same as I saw it written at the christening of her child. Woe's me! 'twas the last time almost I saw her."

"And you believe it was a good marriage?"

"Where's he that says it was not? My Michael? Na, na; 'tis some of them that murdered her. But they cannot get quit of the blood. The young squire would break the connection, would he? Na, na; it was a good marriage, and the ties are too strong."

"Pray, madam," the plaintiff's leader now asked, "did anything particular happen on this occasion?"

"I dinna understand it at all."

"Did you not notice something ... about the ring?"

"Well, the minister was nervous-like, and dropped it, and I said it was no a sign of luck. But I dinna understand it at all."

"Did you know the person whom you call minister, madam?"

"Know him! he was living like at Dame Sennor's, away on the cliff. So they told me."

"Where is Mrs. Sennor now? Is she here?"

"Why, sir, Dame Sennor's been dead and gone this many a year."

"Had you ever seen the minister before the ceremony?"

"I canna say that I had. But he married my Margaret, and that I am well certain."

"How long did your daughter survive afterwards, madam?"

"A little better than three years. But it was a long time sin' I had seen her."

"You used the word 'murdered.' What did you mean, ma'am?"

"Her bliss was made her bane," Maud answered fiercely. "The squire broke her heart, and none of hers were let to come nigh her."

Neither side, it may be observed, chose to confront the old woman with Everope, and inquire concerning her recognition of him. But the judge now desired him to stand forward.

"Look at that person, madam," said his lordship. "Can you say whether that is the man who performed this marriage?"

"Well, I canna tell at all," was the reply. "It's three-and-twenty years agone, and my eyes grow dimly like. I canna tell at all."

Polydore Riches was the next witness. He proved Mr. Trevethlan's urgent request to him to perform the ceremony, and his refusal; that Margaret had always been treated as the mistress of the castle; and that her children had been by him duly christened as the offspring of Henry and Margaret Trevethlan. He also deposed to the behaviour of her relations; to the anger it produced in Mr. Trevethlan; to their banishment from the castle, and their undisguised mortification. In cross-examination he stated, as his reason for refusing to celebrate the union, that he disapproved both of itself and of its manner.

"I must ask you, Mr. Riches, were there not rumours very prevalent soon after the alleged marriage, that it had not been duly performed?"

The question was objected to, but allowed, and the chaplain acknowledged that it was so.

"Did you know this Theodore Ashton, Mr. Riches?"

"Very slightly indeed."

"Are you aware of anything in his character which might make the conduct imputed to him to-day not improbable?"

This question was also objected to, and not pressed.

"Would you have remained an hour in the castle, Mr. Riches," Rereworth then asked; "had you suspected there was anything fraudulent in the marriage?"

"Most certainly I would not."

Griffith and his wife corroborated the evidence of the chaplain, but were also obliged to admit the popular rumours. The licence for the marriage, and also Mr. Trevethlan's will were put in evidence, and then with some other testimony of less consequence, the case for the defence closed. The plaintiff's counsel rose to reply.

In the first place, he begged the jury to disabuse their minds of the imputations which his learned friend had dexterously cast upon some of the evidence in the case. It was rather strange that he should have to defend a witness on the other side, but he was sure they would agree with him, that any indignation on the part of young Sinson would be more than justified, by conduct such as had been vaguely hinted at by his grandmother; and would be properly uncontrollable if the family participated in the popular idea, that the marriage was fraudulent. Their reasons for concealing such suspicions from the pretended bride's mother were evident enough. Her strong feeling was alone an explanation. Then as to Everope, not the least portion of his learned friend's insinuations had been borne out. Whatever might be that person's circumstances, he maintained that no slur had been thrown upon the honesty of his testimony. Now let them look at the presumptions raised for the defence, and see how easily they could be made to tally with the truth of the plaintiff's case. First, there was Mr. Trevethlan's request to his chaplain; why, he would know beforehand, from that gentleman's character, that he would refuse to perform the ceremony. He ran no risk in making the demand, and had it been acceded to, it might have been evaded. Then as to the establishment of Margaret as his wife, it was a mere matter of course, even if it were but temporary. And with regard to his recognition of her children, that was the object of the entire scheme. But it was urged, that he had himself defeated this object. So men often did. Mr. Trevethlan might have feared to expose his conduct at the pretended marriage; he might suppose that the disappearance of Ashton and Wyley would prevent the fraud from being discovered; or he might even, as had been done here to-day, attempt to prove that the mock-marriage was valid. The penalty which hung over the real performer of the ceremony would prevent that person from coming forward. As to the omission in the will, it was probably the effect of long tranquillity and habit. True, the inmates of the castle declared their positive belief in the absence of any deceit; but the jury, and he did not mean it offensively, would recollect their prejudices, and also that even they were compelled to allow that the same feeling did not exist outside the castle walls. Admitting everything that had been proved for the defence, there was nothing inconsistent with the story related by Everope, and confirmed they would recollect by Maud Basset's statement with respect to the ring. And he confidently looked to the jury, not to allow the mere opinions and presumptions of interested parties to outweigh the clear and positive declaration of an indifferent stranger.

Such is a brief narrative of the arguments and evidence adduced on each side, in a trial which in fact occupied many hours. The judge now proceeded to sum up the whole for the consideration of the jury. The court had been densely crowded all day, and the excitement of the audience ran very high.

Whatever difficulty, his lordship gravely remarked, there might be in this case, arose from the deplorable manner in which the late Mr. Trevethlan had caused his marriage to be solemnised, supposing for a moment that it was a marriage. He fully agreed with the reverend witness, Mr. Riches, in entirely condemning such a mode of celebration. Marriages should be performed in public. But the plaintiff denied that there had been any marriage at all, and produced an individual, who swore that not being in holy orders, he took upon himself to read the matrimonial service from the Prayer-book, and falsely and illegally to pronounce Henry Trevethlan and Margaret Basset to be man and wife. If the jury believed that witness, they must return a verdict for the plaintiff, for it was not pretended that there had been any other performance of the rite, than that to which this account would apply. On the other hand, they had heard the evidence adduced to show, that Mr. Trevethlan had always considered his marriage as valid, and that it had been likewise so regarded by all who were connected with his family. But then, again, it would seem that in the neighbourhood a very different opinion had prevailed. Unquestionably the circumstances were mysterious, and he could not but imagine that further evidence would be discovered before very long. With that, however, they had nothing to do. They had to compare a plain and positive story with a strong presumption, and if they were unable to disbelieve the former, to return a verdict, as he had said before, for the plaintiff.

His lordship then went minutely through the evidence on both sides, not sparing the character of Everope, who, he remarked, would certainly have been transported if he had been discovered to have really acted as he confessed, within a certain time now unfortunately elapsed; and, finally, he desired the jury to consider their verdict.

They requested permission to retire; and while they were absent, the excitement of the audience rose to the highest pitch. There was a general buzz of conversation. Every one was speculating on the result. Bets were offered and taken freely. The bar were discussing the judge's charge, and its tendency. Not a few people moved from their places to try to obtain another sight of the defendant. None of the claimant's family were in court. Randolph, perfectly unconscious of the attention he attracted, sat like a statue. His leading counsel looked anxious, and Rereworth lent his forehead on his hands, and seemed to pore over his brief.

"Silence! order!" proclaimed the return of the jury; and the demand did not require to be repeated.

"For the plaintiff," the foreman said, in answer to the question of the clerk of assize.

"May we have immediate possession, my lord?" counsel asked.

The judge shook his head.

There was a rush from the court. It was all over.

CHAPTER XIV.

Thou hast it now, King, Cawdor, Glamis, all;
As the weird women promised; and I fear
Thou play'dst most foully for't: yet it was said,
It should not stand in thy posterity;
But that myself should be the root, and father
Of many kings.

SHAKSPEARE.

That there was much talk, and not a little difference of opinion in the various coteries of Bodmin that night, respecting the issue of the day's proceedings, needs hardly be told. In such cases the crowd can hardly be said to follow fortune and hate the fallen. The jury comes from among it; there is plenty of food for vanity in running down the verdict, and showing how much more rationally matters would have gone if *I* had been one of the twelve. The first gush of popular feeling is generally against the decision in a doubtful case. So here, if there were plenty of suspicion attaching to Henry Trevethlan's marriage, there were also good grounds for discrediting the testimony of Everope. If, on the one hand, scandalized gossips expressed their horror at such clandestine unions, on the other, there was a general cry of indignation at the witness's effrontery. If some people dwelt upon Maud Basset's hints that her daughter was ill-used, others maintained that the mother could not have been deceived at the wedding. If the popular rumours were cited in support of the verdict, they were met by the authority of Polydore Riches. In short, "there was a great deal to be said on both sides." People had an opportunity of showing their discernment, and the majority were apt to flatter their own shrewdness by dissenting from the jury.

He whom it most concerned, was already far from their councils. Randolph left the court immediately on hearing the judgment, with the idea that what had happened was exactly what he had expected, walked hurriedly to his hotel, and ordered out his chaise. Polydore came up to him, and took his hand, and besought him to stay, without extracting a single word in reply. When the chaise drove up, his old pupil merely ejaculated—"I must take the news to Helen. This is the last night either of us sleeps in Trevethlan castle,"—sprang into the vehicle, desired to be driven very fast, and was whirled away, leaving the good chaplain in a state of utter dismay.

Mr. Riches had, however, to rouse himself subsequently, to attend a conference which Winter had arranged for rather a late hour, and at which the counsel for the defendant and Griffith were to assist. The result of the meeting was unsatisfactory. The only practical suggestion was to track Everope's career as closely as possible. It was just within the bounds of probability that they might be able to overthrow that remarkable pedestrian tour; or they might light on other facts tending to elucidate his connection with Michael Sinson; or at least might further damnify his general character. But it was admitted that to chance they must look as their best friend. Time or fortune might bring to knowledge the fate of Mr. Ashton, supposing that he had not been murdered; or again, the missing Wyley might be discovered. Yet of what avail could this last contingency prove, since the witness might have been deceived in the same way as the mother? For the present, there appeared to be no clue to the maze. If the parties would only quarrel, there might indeed be an exposure; but they seemed to be too deeply involved in one another's safety for this event to be at all likely.

Sinson took very good care, in the disquietude of his suspicious temper, that his bondman should not be left in the way of temptation. He started with Everope for London, within a few hours of the termination of the trial. In that wretched man remorse seemed for a time to be dead. Hitherto, in the midst of his lowest depravity, he had always experienced compunctious visitings; he had been always haunted by a sense of forfeited respectability; and had frequently felt a feeble desire to reform. But now, although startled for a moment by the identity of Morton with the defendant, he gladly accepted his position as irremediable, and was looking eagerly for the reward which should furnish him with the means of forgetting it.

But it behoved Michael to keep a strong hold on him for a short time. A very short time, Sinson thought, in the first flush of his triumph, would be sufficient. A few days might put him in possession of all his desires: after that, what became of Everope, or what disclosures he might choose to make, would be a matter of second-rate consequence. Michael felt a kind of admiration for his victim, when he remembered how successfully he had encountered that searching cross-examination. But he could not allow so much ability to run too loose, and resolved to hold him in by drawing his purse-strings very tight, until his own game was perfectly secure.

That it would soon be so, he did not feel the least doubt. He had been playing for weeks and weeks; he had kept his eye steadily fixed upon one event; all his calculations terminated in one result; he had taught himself completely to ignore all unfavourable chances; supposing he had any confidants, he would have regarded their suggestion of difficulty as an insult; he might be thought to fancy that the book of fate lay open before him, and all he read was his own triumph.

And his patroness, she who, in the halls of Pendarrel, was pursuing a line of policy totally at variance with that of her protégé, little dreaming that what seemed to be her victory was intended to be his, utterly unconscious of the price about to be demanded for it—how would she receive the news? Her husband, engaged all day in hearing the details of petty felonies, was discharged with the rest of his colleagues at its close, and retired to recreate himself in their company at a well-served board. There he received the intelligence of the verdict, and accepted the felicitations of his friends. Thence, knowing the penalty which would otherwise await him at home, he withdrew for a little space to indite a despatch for his wife; and then, having entrusted the missive to a trusty rider, with injunctions to lose no time on the road, he was able to rejoin his friends before the decanters had completed their first round.

So the news was ready for the mistress of Pendarrel by breakfast-time. In the first flush of exultation she made her daughter a partner in it.

"Mildred, my love, I give you joy. You are heiress of Trevethlan Castle."

But the young lady regarded her mother with a countenance in which there were no signs of joy, and the for once imprudent parent bit her lip.

"And my cousins," Mildred said, "are ruined."

"They are no cousins of yours, child," said her mother, not yet having regained perfect presence of mind; "nor of any one else. Nor are they ruined. I shall take good care of that."

Mrs. Pendarrel would very gladly have recalled the remark which had excited her daughter's sympathy, in order to convey the information in a tone of less unqualified satisfaction. But she forgot her wariness in the pride occasioned by the success of all her long machinations.

"Pendar'l and Trevethlan would own one name."

And that name would be Pendarrel. Nay, more; the name of Trevethlan would vanish from the earth. The family would sink into oblivion. If he who had slighted her could rise from his grave, and see the ruin which had followed his scorn; could see how his towers had passed into the hands of his foe; how his fame was blighted, and his children dishonoured; were there not ample satisfaction for all the long misery his contempt had inflicted? "No!" Esther was compelled to answer, as that eternal spring of bitter waters burst forth amidst the sweet flood of revenge. "No, nothing can compensate me for the sorrow which conscience whispers has been due to my own arrogance; nothing can atone for the wreck of that happiness, which, but for my own presumption, might have been mine."

Reflections like these, however, were soon crushed, and Mrs. Pendarrel had quite sufficient employment on her hands. Since the night of her great party, she had been assiduously pressing forward the preparations for Mildred's marriage. Perfectly heedless of the attitude assumed by the young lady, she was arranging all the details of the affair with maternal diligence, and had gone so far as to select the persons who were to be present at the ceremony. Mr. Truby had been himself to the Hall to receive final instructions respecting the settlements. Melcomb was an assiduous visitor, but by no means solicitous for *tête-à-têtes* with his intended bride. To him the marriage was become nearly a matter of life and death. It was true the gossips at Mrs. Pendarrel's party had somewhat exaggerated his embarrassments; but his creditors were growing very importunate, and impatiently awaiting the day when the possession of his wife's fortune would enable him to satisfy their most pressing demands: a purpose to which he had undertaken it should be devoted. Let it be rumoured that the match was broken off, and it might not be very long before Tolpeden Park suffered the outrages alluded to by Mr. Quitch. So Melcomb disguised whatever inward anxiety he might feel, under a smooth brow and a smiling face, and evaded his mistress's repugnance as best he might.

Mildred's remonstrances had subsided into passive resistance. She was generally silent and calm. The irksomeness of her situation was greatly aggravated; but, at the same time, her spirit was sustained by the memory which she cherished in her heart of the scene under the hawthorns of the cliff. Trusting that some accident might even yet frustrate her mother's intentions, she allowed her to proceed without protest, acting on her sister's advice, to postpone éclat to the latest possible period. She felt that she had deceived no one, and, if scandal came, it would be no fault of hers.

But had Esther been fully aware of all that was fermenting in the young lady's mind, she would, indeed, have bit her lips hard, rather than let slip that intimation respecting Trevethlan Castle. The idea of flight had occurred to the reluctant maiden more than once; coming, however, only to be dismissed. But if her lover were really ruined, if he to whom she had plighted herself were an exile from house and home, forlorn and outcast, then it was not unlikely Mildred might think that her vow as well as her affection bade her seek him, at once to share and to console his sorrow.

So Mrs. Pendarrel's hasty exclamation brought distress and anxiety to her daughter, and imparted a certain consistency to a notion which had previously been shadowy as a dream. Mildred wrote a long letter to her sister, partly lifting the veil from the emotions which agitated her, and dwelling more strongly than she had ever done before, upon the disquietude she felt at the mode in which the match was being hurried forward.

But it was not from this communication that Mrs. Winston would learn the result of the law-suit. She was at a party, when she overheard an allusion to it from a bystander. He was a barrister, who had been present at the trial, and who, having finished his business at the assizes, had returned with speed to London. She knew the person he was conversing with, joined them, and learned all the particulars. She had before talked the affair over, and was fully aware of the consequences to the orphans of Trevethlan. She immediately quitted the assembly, went home, and interrupted her husband in his studies. A brilliant creature she was, glowing in all the lustre and maturity of thirty summers, and now adorned with everything that could be imagined to enhance her beauty. So she swept to Mr. Winston's side, and laid her hand lightly upon his shoulder. And, with all his love of ease and philosophy, his indolence and affected apathy, he was really proud of his wife, and gratified whenever she came to him with a request. So, if there were a little impatience in his mind, when he looked up from his book into her face, it vanished immediately in admiration, and was succeeded by pleasure when he found she had come to consult him.

"So soon home, Gertrude," he said. "And why? I trust nothing is the matter."

She related what she had heard respecting the law-suit.

"And now," she concluded, "what will become of my unhappy cousins?"

"I think, my dear," her husband said, after some reflection,—"I think there could be no harm, considering all the circumstances, there could be no harm, I imagine, in begging Miss Trevethlan to make our house her home. I do not believe this verdict will stand. But, at all events, we might invite Miss Trevethlan to stay with us; at any rate for a time. She might be as private as she pleased. What do you say, my dear? You might write to her...."

He had laid his open volume upon his knee. What he suggested was precisely what Mrs. Winston desired. So much coldness had attended all her intercourse with her mother, since their last discussion about Mildred's marriage, that she took no heed of any objection from that quarter. She answered her husband by bending down and touching his cheek with her lips. He thought she had never looked so beautiful before, and threw away his book.

That evening was the beginning of a new era in Gertrude's life.

CHAPTER XV.

Desdichada fué la hora,
Desdichado fué aquel dia
En que naci y heredé
La tau grande senoria;
Pues lo habia de perder
Todo junto y en un dia.

ROMAN. ESPAN.

Late in the night, or early in the morning that followed the trial at Bodmin, any watcher at Trevethlan would be startled by the gallop of horses and the rattle of wheels, as the chaise which bore Randolph to his lost home dashed round the green of the hamlet. The bell rung loud at the castle-gate, and old Jeffrey roused himself from his slumbers, and having looked to the state of his blunderbus, descended leisurely to learn who sought admission at that untimely hour. His master's voice impatiently ordered him to open the gate; and, with a wonder that impeded his duty, he obeyed. Delay again occurred before Randolph obtained entrance to the great hall; and when he did, the white face upon which fell the glare of the trembling handmaiden's lamp, might remind her of those sheeted spectres which were said to glide at that hour through the desolate corridors. He bade her leave him a light, and she fled, scared, back to the couch from which she had unwillingly risen.

Randolph strode with irregular steps up and down the vaulted hall. Perhaps, had Griffith been there, the worthy steward would have remembered the day when his late master paced it in the like manner, after his furious ride from Pendarrel. He might recollect the same fierce passion in his eye—the same dark scowl upon his forehead, as those which now burnt and loured in the face of his son. Nor were it very easy to say which had sustained the greatest provocation: the father, led on and enchained in a deep attachment, only to feel himself the sport of a wayward girl's vanity; or the son, who found the same girl, now a woman, triumphing in that father's dishonour, and exulting over the ruin of his house. And that was not all, for the disgrace descended: the good name, which had been handed down from generation to generation, almost from beyond the memory of man, with him, Randolph—what?—was changed into an inheritance of shame. And he too loved. He loved the child of his destroyer. He had sometimes rejoiced in the idea of wreaking the vengeance bequeathed to him, by stealing her from her mother. For she also loved him, and had vowed to be his. And now;—what was to happen now? Ruin, privation, poverty, he might have invited her to share, while honour was unstained. But could he ask her to join the fortunes of one who had not even a name to offer her? The reputed offspring of fraud and sin? Never, while there remained a shadow in which calumny might wrap itself—never, while there was a suspicion upon which envy might pretend to believe the tale related that day—could he accept the fulfilment of his beloved one's promise.

And what hope was there? Had he not swept the dark horizon again and again in search of the faintest ray of light, and failed to discover any? And if his vision, sharpened by despair, could discover none, whose could? Had he not listened to every syllable of the foul tale, with the ears of one who sought a flaw in his death-warrant? And had he been able to discover any? Then if he were deaf, who could hear?

And this was the story with which he must greet his sister in the morning. For delay, dalliance with chance was out of the question. As he had told Polydore Riches, not another night should the castle find him beneath its roof. Speedy possession! It had been refused, but they might take it. He would not remain where his very name seemed to mock him.

Therefore he and Helen were in fact houseless. Well, they would again seek their old quarters near the metropolis. They still possessed a few months' maintenance. Afterwards, let what would happen, it would not much matter.

These bitter thoughts occupied Randolph when the grey light of day-break stole through the lofty casements, and reminded him of the necessity of repose. He sought his own chamber. The sea lay beneath him, calm and still, but without its usual tranquillising influence. Dressed as he was he flung himself upon his bed, and sheer exhaustion brought some fitful slumber.

The sun was shining bright into the room, when he finally awoke. His morning orisons, never neglected, inspired him with something like resignation. He would not, indeed, remain a day at the castle, but he would only go to London to be near head-quarters, and avail himself of the best assistance in unveiling the iniquity by which for a season he had been defeated. And, animated by this determination, he met his sister at breakfast with a countenance which told plainly enough what had happened, but at the same time was not utterly devoid of hope; one, "wherein appeared, obscure, some glimpse of joy."

"It is against us, my brother," Helen said, when the repast was over.

"Ay, Helen," he answered. "We are outcasts upon earth, from our home, and from our name. There is nothing left us but to say farewell. We may as well say it immediately. Can you be ready to depart this very day?"

He saw that his sister's eyes were filled with tears.

"It is sudden, dearest," he said; "but it is better so. I cannot stay here, while a taint rests upon my name. We can travel to-day, and what we want may follow us. And it will not be 'a farewell for ever.'"

He smiled as he spoke, but he could win no corresponding glance from Helen. They separated to make the necessary preparations for departure.

It was not much past noon, when the friends arrived whom Randolph had left at Bodmin. They united in protesting against the projected journey. But argument was vain. Randolph had completed his plan. He should go straight to his old quarters at Hampstead; that is, if he found them unoccupied; should put himself in close communication with Winter and his friend Rereworth; and follow up an inquiry into the evidence given at the trial with untiring energy. If such investigation were fruitless—but he was not inclined to accept that alternative—he need hardly say, that not for an hour would he waive his claim to the name of Trevethlan, and that therefore he had no notion of resuming his old disguise. He had no objection to Griffith remaining at the castle as long as the law would permit, but he earnestly pressed the chaplain to follow him to the metropolis.

"You will be such a support to my sister, Mr. Riches," he urged. "I shall be much away from her. Engaged in business; unable to sustain her in this great change. Do come, my dear sir, and help your old pupils in their extremity."

Polydore was not one to resist such an entreaty, and assented. Yet, perhaps, Randolph might have been prevailed upon at least to defer his departure, but for an invitation to do so from another quarter. A note reached the castle from Mrs. Pendarrel, in which that lady expressed her hope that its present occupants would put themselves to no inconvenience; that the demand for immediate possession was unauthorized, and that every accommodation would be granted with pleasure. This polite missive, it may be presumed, was in partial fulfilment of the intention Esther expressed to her daughter, of assisting her adversaries in their fall. But it was too much like that which she caused her husband to write in the opening of this narrative, to be received as a favour, and only served to provoke Randolph into a fresh burst of rage, and make him eager for the vehicle which should bear them away from all such insults.

Before it came, however, he could not resist guiding his sister to a last visit to the haunt of their childhood, Merlin's Cave. And there for no little space they sat in silence, thinking over the happiness of by-gone days. The day was even warmer than those which had preceded it, but it was close and heavy. The sea lay before the orphans, perfectly smooth, sleeping in its might; and there was no breath of air to waft aside the lightest bubble it might leave upon the rock; but some round massive clouds were rising one behind another in the south-western horizon, which might indicate the coming of a storm.

"Farewell to Trevethlan!" Randolph said. "Let me hear our old song once more."

And Helen sang the ancestral ditty, but with an accent very different from that she gave it on the eve of their previous journey to the metropolis.

"Farewell to Trevethlan! A farewell for ever!Farewell to the towers that stand by the sea!"

"Remember, Helen," her brother said, "how you checked me when I told you your song was of ill omen. And believe me now, when I say that, like Reginald, we shall live to see a joyful revolution."

Ill news flies fast. The intelligence of the verdict had spread in the hamlet, and its immediate effect was exaggerated by the villagers. The coming departure of their young master and mistress also travelled from the castle to the green, and added to the excitement. Groups collected both of sorrowing women and of threatening men. The lapse of time only increased the numbers and the exasperation of the tenantry. The people speedily forgot all those rumours concerning their late lord's marriage, which of old gratified their envy, and which had probably contributed in no small degree to the result of the trial. They only considered the event of the day; that the last representative of the family with which they had been connected for centuries was now to be driven from his home, by a deserter who had sold himself to a rival house; and many among them resolved, that if they could prevent it, by right or wrong, it should not be so that "Pendar'l and Trevethlan should own one name."

"And so ye were right after all, dame," said farmer Colan to the landlady of the Trevethlan Arms. "The old saying's come true with a vengeance. But there's no Miss Mildred in the case."

"And Madam Pendarrel's not come to Trevethlan yet, farmer," was the answer. "And there's many a slip 'twixt the cup and the lip."

"There's like to be a slip here," cried a voice in the crowd, "such as she little knows."

"It's a curious sort of day for the season," said Breage. "So warm and heavy. I should say there was some prognostication in the air."

"Ay, there'll be a storm before long, I reckon, neighbours," said Germoe.

"Faith, then, there will," muttered another speaker; "and a storm some people don't expect."

"There always is a storm," observed the general merchant, "along with misfortune at the castle. It comes as a token."

"Then it comes too late," quoth Mrs. Miniver. "It is after the misfortune this time. Who knows what came of Michael Sinson?"

A low groan ran through the throng, and filled the eyes of Mercy Page with tears.

"What'll his old grandame say," asked farmer Colan, "when she understands the rights of the matter?"

"She never will understand," answered the hostess. "She'll close her ears, and say it is all along of squire Randolph. Don't ye mind how she met him at the late master's burying? And how she says that her Margaret was murdered?"

"'T is a strange thing," remarked the village tailor, "that nothing ever turned up about the parson's murder."

"He never was murdered," said Breage; "if he had, there'd have been a sign. I don't believe as he was murdered."

The appearance of an empty carriage, winding its way round the green, put an end to these gossiping speculations, and concentrated the scattered groups of rustics into one compact crowd about the gate leading into the base-court of the castle. A moody silence succeeded to the previous animation, and all eyes followed the vehicle up the ascent, until it vanished from sight through the arched portal. Even the mirthful Mrs. Miniver then became serious for once, and waited among her neighbours in rueful anxiety for the re-appearance of the carriage.

We pass lightly over the adieux within the inner court. Polydore Riches, having resigned himself to what was inevitable, made them as brief as possible. Randolph had steeled his heart against any display of feeling, and Helen endeavoured to imitate her brother's fortitude. The steward found comfort in hope; but his wife could not restrain her sorrow at such a parting, and retired to the picture-gallery to try to forget the present disaster, in calling to mind the past glories of the family to which she was so deeply attached. Old Jeffrey flung open the gates, and dashed a tear surlily from his eye as the carriage passed under the arch. But when the family flag was seen slowly and lingeringly to descend from its high place, a wailing cry arose from the crowd upon the green, which made Randolph's heart swell in his breast, and brought the tears she had resolved not to shed into Helen's eyes.

The carriage soon reached the bottom of the descent. The people thronged to the gate, and pressed against it, and loudly declared that it should not be opened. Not so would they allow their young master and mistress to be taken from them. There was considerable confusion, and cries were uttered expressive of the villagers' determination. The driver, perplexed, looked round for instructions. The situation was becoming embarrassing.

"We will bid our friends farewell on foot, Helen," her brother whispered, "and thank them for their good-will."

And, so saying, he threw open his door of the carriage, sprang out, lowered the steps himself, and assisted his sister to alight. She leant upon his arm, and they advanced to meet the crowd, which divided before them with great respect. Shaking hands very cordially with those who were nearest them, and expressing confident hopes that their absence would not be long, they made their way across the green, while the carriage proceeded by the road. But the people soon divined their intention, and closed upon their path, and endeavoured to delay their progress, clasping their hands, and pouring benedictions upon their heads. It was a more trying leave-taking than that within the castle. But at length, after many and many a salute, they reached the end of the village, re-ascended their carriage amid renewed effusions of attachment, and were borne rapidly from the sight of their sorrowing adherents.

Sorrow, however, was not the only emotion excited by their departure. Not a few imprecations, fiercely directed against the house that had disinherited them, arose among their dependents as the carriage finally disappeared.

END OF VOLUME II.